THE FULFILMENT OF A DREAM OF PASTOR HSI'S

THE FULFILMENT
of
A Dream
of
PASTOR HSI'S

THE STORY OF THE WORK IN HWOCHOW

by
A. MILDRED CABLE
Of the China Inland Mission

SCRIPTURE TESTIMONY EDITION

WALKING TOGETHER PRESS
ESTES PARK · JENTA MANGORO

About the cover: This image depicts a group of opium addicts seeking help at a mission hospital. While these particular men are not mentioned in this book, they represent a typical scene.

This image is in the public domain.

Opium smokers under cure: Chaochowfoo. 1906.
https://impa.usc.edu/asset-management/2A3BF1D6AZCE

Colorized by Jacoba Looije

Published in 2025 by
Walking Together Press
Estes Park, Colorado USA
Jenta Mangoro, Jos, Plateau Nigeria
walkingtogether.press

Print ISBN: 978-1-961568-39-6
eBook ISBN: 978-1-961568-40-2

Cover design by D. Thaine Norris
Typeset in Adobe Garamond Pro by Kurdor Peter

1

ABOUT THE SCRIPTURE TESTIMONY EDITION

IN *The Fulfilment of a Dream of Pastor Hsi's,* Mildred Cable weaves a narrative that is both engaging and spiritual. With remarkable skill, she transports the reader to early 20th-century Hwochow, China, painting a vivid picture of missionary life filled with miracles, joys, sorrows, and challenges. Her keen eye for detail and deep empathy allow the reader to truly experience the pulse of Hwochow—its people, traditions, and the transformative power of the message of Jesus Christ.

At its heart, this book is a powerful testament to the boundless impact of Christian faith. Cable shares timeless spiritual truths with the reader: the awe-inspiring power of faith, the revolutionary power of loving one's enemies, all powered by the gospel's unparalleled ability to renew hearts and minds. And with unflinching honesty, she also explores the ever-present Christian struggle against temptation, reminding the reader of the vigilance required in the God-ward journey. We believe that as you turn the final page, you will find yourself not only enlightened about a fascinating chapter in Christian history but also spiritually enriched.

Data science reveals trends and patterns in information. The *Scripture Testimony Index* is an extensive research project using artificial intelligence and data science to develop a New-Testament-driven subject index across a large body of missionary biographies and personal narratives. As the story enthusiasts at Walking Together Press study these books programmatically; beautiful, bright threads emerge—threads of prayer, provision, deliverance, specific leading, healing, transformation, revival, and miraculous conversion. The end result is an index of thousands of short story excerpts organized by subject and Bible verse that empirically demonstrate the truth of the Scriptures, and which is freely available on our website at walkingtogether.life. Another result of this research was the discovery of dozens of great books that are long out of print and in danger of being forgotten. The *Scripture Testimony Collection* is a set of such books that we enthusiastically recommend, to the degree that we are making the effort to republish them.

Walking Together Press has enhanced this classic title, *The Fulfilment of a Dream of Pastor Hsi's,* by identifying and marking twenty-three portions of the narrative that illustrate specific Biblical topics and verses. An extensive *Scripture Testimony Index* has also been added containing short summaries of how each Scriptural topic is illustrated, making locating specific stories easy. Furthermore, this title is one of many in the *Scripture Testimony Collection.*

TO

DR. G. CAMPBELL MORGAN

THE "APOLLOS" WHO

BY PRAYER AND SYMPATHY HAS "WATERED"

THIS WORK

THIS BOOK IS AFFECTIONATELY DEDICATED

INTRODUCTION

TWENTY-ONE YEARS ago, on 19th February 1896, Pastor Hsi, to quote the words of his biographer, "was translated to higher service." Those who read the fascinating and wonderful story of his life by Mrs. Howard Taylor will at once be interested in *The Fulfilment of a Dream*, which is the story of the work in Hwochow, and gives the account of the carrying on of the spiritual labour of that remarkable man, and of the fulfilment of his dream. I think it is equally true that those who have not read Pastor Hsi's life will desire to do so after reading this book.

It is a commonplace observation, but none the less true, that the story commenced in the Acts of the Apostles could not be finished by Luke, because the great activity, the commencement of which he recorded, is still going forward. Every tale of missionary endeavour moving forward "toward the uttermost part of the earth" is an added chapter. It has been given to Mildred Cable and her fellow workers, to labour in the apostolic succession; and then to Mildred Cable, to write this wonderful chapter.

From my own standpoint the book is full of charm. While by no means its supreme value, the first impression made upon the mind is that of the naturalness of the story. The reader is made the friend of the writer, and listens to an artless and charming account of places and of peoples. My first reading of the book at one sitting (as all such books should be read), left me with a sense of the atmosphere of the missionary's life and surroundings. I was admitted into the actuality of everyday things, and was made familiar with the pathos and tragedy and humour of life in a land and among a people largely unknown to me.

As I have said, this is by no means the supreme value of the book. That rather consists in something that grows upon you as you read. The writer does not state it in so many words, or very seldom, and certainly is not trying to persuade you to believe it, but there it is. I refer to the tender and yet strong revelation of the power of the Divine Grace, both in its sustenance of those who are called to missionary work, and its transforming power in the case of those who, often at cost, yield themselves to its call.

In Chapters I., V., VI., VII., and VIII. the reader will trace the story of the development of the work, and a wonderful story it is. Chapters XI. and XII., containing first the story of Ai Do, and then a record of demoniacal manifestations, show the reader how these quiet and earnest workers are brought up against the big, naked, awful things of life; and also how being so confronted, they are unafraid and unconquered in the name of Jesus Christ the Lord. The fact that I draw special attention to these chapters is not intended to suggest for a moment that the others are either uninteresting or unimportant. They are neither the one nor the other. For all that it is intended to be, the book is a whole, and is supremely precious, because it is manifestly a part of the larger whole of Christ's great emprise.

With confidence and joy I commend the story to all those in whose heart burns the passion for the coming of the hour when our adorable Redeemer shall "see of the travail of His soul, and shall be satisfied."

G. CAMPBELL MORGAN.

AUTHOR'S PREFACE

I wish to acknowledge that apart from my coworkers, Evangeline and Francesca French, this book would have been impossible. To Mr. Albert Lutley, Superintendent of the China Inland Mission Work in the Province of Shansi, I am indebted for help and kindnesses which I can acknowledge, but never repay. I am also indebted to my Chinese secretary, Miss Wang, for her able reporting of the many interviews which the compiling of this book has necessitated.

The Chinese themselves say: "One mile alters the speech, and ten miles change the customs."

In view of the fact that the Province of Shansi alone is larger than England and Wales, I wish it to be clearly understood that the usages and customs to which I refer throughout this book are local.

EDITOR'S NOTE

ALL PERSONAL names are spelt according to the system employed by the authoress, except where it has been necessary to modify this to retain the identity of someone mentioned in Mrs. Howard Taylor's *Pastor Hsi*. All place names are spelt according to the orthography of the Chinese Postal Guide, which system is now used in the standard maps of China and has been adopted by the larger missionary societies. Thus, Hoh-chau of *Pastor Hsi* becomes Hwochow, T'ai-yüan becomes Taiyüanfu, P'ing-yang becomes Pingyangfu, etc.

CONTENTS

PROLOGUE

THE SPIRIT of the Confucian scholar Hsi met with its Master Christ, and overwhelmed by the vision yielded all to His control. Constrained by His love the souls of men were sought

and won; led by His Spirit, churches were established in the faith; sharing His sufferings, their failures became his burden.

In the darkest days the Hwochow Church has known, when many forsook their faith, he was strengthened by a dream, in which he saw a tree cut down to the ground, only to sprout again, and throw out branches stronger than before.

In his dream, Pastor Hsi knew this tree to be the Hwochow Church. He knew that though it were brought low, it would revive, and by faith obtained the promise, the fulfilment of which is recorded in these pages.

When Thou wouldst pour the Living Stream
Then I would be the earthen cup,
Filled to the brim and sparkling clear.
The Fountain Thou and Living Spring
Flow Thou through me, the vessel weak,
That thirsty souls may taste Thy grace.

When Thou wouldst warn the people, Lord,
Then I would be the golden bell
Swung high athwart the lofty tower
Morning and evening sounding loud;
That young and old may wake from sleep,
Yea, e'en the deaf hear that strong sound.

When Thou wouldst light the darkness, Lord,
Then I would be the silver lamp
Whose oil supply can never fail.
Placed high, to shed the beams afar,
That darkness may be turned to light,
And men and women see Thy face.

When Thou wouldst slay the wolves, O Lord
Then I would be the keen-edged sword;
Clean, free from rust, sharpened and sure,
The handle grasped, my God, by Thee.
To kill the cruel, ravening foe,
And save the sheep for whom Christ died.

Translated from Pastor Hsi by F. L. F.

MRS. HSI'S GIFT

"First love is the abandonment of all for the love which has abandoned all."—Dr. G. Campbell Morgan.
. . such men
Carry the fire, all things grow warm to them.
Their drugget's worth my purple, they beat me."
R. Browning.

CHAPTER I

MRS. HSI'S GIFT

BEING AN ACCOUNT OF THE OPENING
OF THE STATION OF HWOCHOW

MRS. HSI was in great mental distress. The blow she feared had fallen, and her husband was a prey to the bewitching power of the "foreign devils." How cleverly the trap had been laid. Firstly, the offer of a monetary prize for a classical essay—which he had won; secondly, the insistence of the foreigner on a personal interview with the writer, on the occasion of which, certain as her husband had been that he had tasted neither food nor drink under his roof, some means had certainly been found to introduce into his system some of that subtle foreign drug which, as every one knew, must eventually compel the victim to embrace Christianity and follow the "foreign devil" to the world's end. Thirdly, he had been invited to become the teacher of this dreaded man (Rev. David Hill), and she had foolishly yielded her consent. She had taken every precaution and had, on three occasions, sent for him on plea of her own illness during the time he was an inmate in the foreigner's household. His clothing had been carefully searched for traces of the magical compound, but in vain; nothing had come to light, and now here was her husband, one of the leading Confucianists of the district, declaring that, of his own free will and action, he had determined to follow — not the foreign devils—but this Jesus, around Whom all their preaching centred. He attributed this change of mind, evidently quite irrationally, to the reading of a book printed under the strange title of *Happy Sound*,—but perhaps even the sacred Chinese character might become a snare in their hands! Nothing but the influence of some powerful magic could have worked so complete a transformation. Even his intense craving for opium was gone, the Confucian writings which had been his constant companion were now neglected, and in spite of her entreaties and fears, the family gods were destroyed.

During his stay at home he spoke constantly, both to her and in her hearing to many visitors, of the teachings of this Jesus Who, he explained to all comers, was the Son of the only True God.

*　　*　　*　　*　　*　　*　　*　　*　　*

> **SCRIPTURE TESTIMONY**
>
> *In Christ, believers are free from bondage*
>
> ROMANS 14:22 · GALATIANS 5:1 · GALATIANS 6:10

Time passed, and gradually her fears were somewhat allayed, so that she even consented to repeat certain sentences which, he told her, were to be used night and morning, kneeling, and with closed eyes. Her inclination to favourably regard what he told her grew, especially during his absences from home; for, strange to relate, she soon began to find herself under the influence of an unaccountable external power, which compelled her on each occasion of a visit from her husband to fly into an uncontrollable rage at the sight of him, and this despite her most determined resolution to the contrary. To her husband it was most distressing to see so gentle a woman thus transformed. As his own spiritual experience increased, he recognised in this an onslaught of the devil, and betook himself to prayer and fasting in order to discover how they had laid themselves open to the attack. It was then that there was brought to his remembrance the fact that, in a room at the top of the house, there stood a small idol responsible for the health of the family, whose existence Mrs. Hsi had been careful not to bring to his remembrance, and which had been overlooked in the general destruction. The shrine was instantly destroyed, and Mrs. Hsi was free of the tormenting spirit, and shortly afterwards openly confessed Christ.

From that time their home in the Western Chang village was a centre of Christian activity. Through intense suffering Mr. Hsi had freed himself from the craving for opium, and he felt that, for the evangelisa-

> **SCRIPTURE TESTIMONY**
>
> *God communicating in a dream*
>
> MATTHEW 1:20 · MATTHEW 2:12
> · MATTHEW 2:13 · MATTHEW 2:19
> · MATTHEW 2:22 · MATTHEW
> 27:19 · ACTS 2:17

tion of his native province, some means might be devised whereby the treatment of opium patients might be combined with widespread preaching of the Gospel.

The more he thought of this the stronger the conviction grew that it was of God, and when, through the agency of a dream, a system of treatment was revealed to him, he accepted it as a revelation and at once prepared the medicine which proved successful beyond his highest expectations. After a time, men who had been delivered from the opium vice and led to Christ through the Refuges, were gathered into his home (which he called the Middle Eden) and trained for the work.

This community life for so large a number was only made possible by Mrs. Hsi's enthusiastic devotion. The extension of the opium refuge work was rapid and widespread, and necessitated frequent absences from home on the part of Mr. Hsi, during which time a heavy burden fell upon his wife.

Houses were rented in many towns and villages, and patients entering the "heavenly called refuges"[1] were numerous.

The burden of one city, however, lay heavily upon the heart of Mr. Hsi, and he and his household constantly prayed together that Hwochow might be opened to the

> **SCRIPTURE TESTIMONY**
>
> *Generously give to those in need*
>
> ACTS 4:32-37 · GALATIANS 6:2 ·
> HEBREWS 13:16 · I JOHN 3:17

sound of the Gospel; but funds which seemed essential for the initial expenses of the venture were not forthcoming. His itinerant journeys frequently took him through this important centre, which was situated

---

1   Heavenly Invitation Office ("Pastor Hsi's" translation)

sixty miles north of his home.

Day after day prayer was made, and Mrs. Hsi often heard her husband in the night watches, as he knelt alone in the court, plead with God that nothing might hinder what he strongly believed to be the Divine Purpose.

One Sunday night she was wakened by the familiar sound. She knew that her husband, like herself, had gone to bed tired out by a long day of preaching, during which large numbers had joined their household from more or less distant villages. According to their custom, they had spent the day fasting; it was Pastor Hsi's habit to refer to the Scriptures direct for guidance on matters of daily conduct, and in the early days of his faith he feared to sin against the law of God by allowing fires to be lighted and meals to be prepared on Sunday. In accordance with his habit, he had arisen soon after midnight to give himself to prayer, and her ear caught the murmured sentences, "I beseech Thee, O Lord, open a way for Hwochow to hear the Gospel." As she listened, the sound of his voice brought conviction to her own mind that she was to be the human agency by which the Divine Will should now fulfil itself. In a flash, the path of duty was clear.

At the back of her cave were large painted cupboards which contained the whole of her worldly possessions: bundles of handsome silk, satin, and embroidered garments, and a box holding the heavy jade and silver ornaments, which had been her husband's marriage gift. Leaving her *kang*[1] Mrs. Hsi unlocked the cupboards and spent the rest of that night in sorting their contents. All except a few cotton gowns were put to one side, and as the voice in the courtyard still pleaded for Hwochow, even the earrings were taken from her ears, the rings from her fingers, and the ornaments from her hair.

He Who is worthy to receive accepted the offering, and her heart sang a song of thanksgiving as she murmured to herself, "Hwochow shall have the Gospel."

Morning prayers at Middle Eden was an hour of joyful worship, and on this day Mrs. Hsi's heart was so full of happiness that she could scarcely wait until the full congregation had assembled before she, laden with her bundles, entered the room and placed them on the table, saying, "I think God has

---

1   The raised brick or mud platform, heated by a fire, used as a bed in North China.

answered our prayers; I can do without these, let Hwochow have the Gospel."

Every heart present must have been moved, for all could judge accurately what the sacrifice must be. She had offered her only worldly treasures, articles which her husband could not ask her to sacrifice, ready as he was to use in God's service all that pertained to their home.

Surely the angels joined their song to that of the little Christian community that morning, as the words of their own pastor's hymn ascended with the sacrifice of praise:

> "I hung for thee on Calvary, what dost thou still withhold
> from Me?
> Thy strength, thy time, thy goods?
> Oh say, what dost thou yet deny,
> My heart of love to satisfy?"

THE BIG ROAD

"Allons I whoever you are, come travel with me!
Travelling with me you find what never tires.
Whoever you are, come forth! a man or a woman,
    come forth!
You must not stay sleeping or dallying there in the house,
  though you built it, or though it has been built for you."

                    Walt Whitman.

"The Master said: With coarse rice to eat, with water to drink,
and my bended arm for a pillow;—I have still joy in the midst of
these things."—*Confucian Analects.*

CHAPTER II

THE BIG ROAD

INDICATING THE SITUATION OF HWOCHOW
IN THE PROVINCE OF SHANSI

THE CITY of Hwochow is situated on the main road which connects Taiyüanfu with Sianfu, the direct route from Peking to the north-western provinces. Along this road pass strings of camels, laden with the merchandise of Mongolia; thousands of donkeys, carrying bags of flour from the more luxuriant southern plains; cartloads of tobacco and paper from the large cities in the south of the province, and caravans of travellers; whole families packed into large carts moving to some new home; mat-covered litters swung between two mules and heavily curtained, in which the wives of an official are transported to their new abode; pedestrians, clad in sky-blue cotton, "*Yamen* runners" yelling as they ride at furious speed to clear the way before them, and bearers of burdens combine to form a moving picture of interest and beauty upon the Big Road, as it is called.

Not least interesting among the wayfarers are the Lhamas from distant Thibet nearing the end of their long pilgrimage to the famous holy mountain Wutai, where each one hopes to be granted the vision of the famous opening lotus. For many months, stretching into years, this hope has

11

sustained them through the weary pilgrimage. From the threshold of their Lhama home they have walked every step of the thousand and more miles, some at every tenth, some at every fifth step, touching the ground with their forehead, and some measuring the whole length of the way with their outstretched body on the road.

As the traveller enters Hwochow from the north, he crosses a bridge, passing on his right a large metal cow. Beyond, flows the Fen River, and before him is the city gate. To this brazen image is committed the important function of guarding Hwochow from flood, and so successfully does it accomplish its task that dryness and drought are the normal condition of the countryside!

Turning to the east he faces the magnificent range of the Ho Mountains, in winter covered with snow, and in warmer seasons touched with the beauty of ever-changing colour. These mountains are part of the range which, farther north, is traversed by the famous Lingshih Pass.

Excepting in the early summer months when patches of vivid green indicate the fields of growing wheat, the landscape is of a uniform shade which is best described as *khaki*. Owing to the friable nature of the soil formation known as *loess*, the traveller, whether journeying from north or south, finds himself in a succession of deep gullies.

This wheat-growing land was formerly given over to the cultivation of the opium poppy, and for miles over the plain the wonderful iridescent bloom gave the appearance of a sea of changing light and shade as the wind passed over it.

In the year 1908 a proclamation was issued forbidding the growth of opium under penalty of death, and so vigorously has the law been enforced that the poppy has completely disappeared from view, and no man is bold enough to openly grow that which has been forbidden by the authorities.

For ten months in the year brilliant sunshine can be counted upon, and during that time, except for dust combined with heat or cold, the physical condition of a journey may be comparatively easy. Ease of mind, however, can only be attained by the philosopher who, putting away all thought of unseemly haste, shares the Easterner's pleasures of observation, contemplation, and wayside intercourse.

The journey from Taiyüanfu to Hwochow is accomplished in five stages, and nothing will induce the carter to shorten or change them, though hours may have been wasted in some narrow gully where, spite his warning yells, his cart met another at a point where advance or retreat on either side were alike impossible. After fierce recriminations the two men each produce a pipe, and it is good practice for the impatient Westerner to see them sit on their heels and talk the matter over. Time passes, but the carter is untrammelled by any artificial measure thereof, and after endless discussion, amid comforting whiffs of tobacco, he proceeds to think of a plan whereby the deadlock may be overcome. How they manage to extricate themselves, one never knows! Some of the bank comes down, yells and shouts do their part, and at last the traffic, which may now amount to fifty waiting carts, slowly passes by. It is an everyday occurrence, and you ask, "Why do they not widen the road?" "Nobody's business," is the reply. "Who would spend the money?"

It is, however, the rainy season that reveals to the full the horrors of Chinese travelling. The *loess* is slippery beyond description, and the litter or cart in which you travel may be stuck for hours in a pit of greasy mud, black by reason of the coal dust so plentiful throughout the district, so deep that nothing but the mule's head is visible, the plunging body being hidden in the black mass. Your only hope at such a moment is to throw yourself with the grace of an expert gymnast on to the bank, thankful if you escape unhurt and only bespattered by mud. These pits are carefully kept in condition by a small group of men who appear, as by magic, to offer assistance at the suitable moment. No plight, however, excites their pity sufficiently to induce them to render help apart from a pecuniary reward of an exorbitant nature. Once within the city gates there is hope that you will soon find a shelter. You will have accomplished "the stage" which has been allotted from time immemorial. Marco Polo himself followed these stages in the year 1280 as we do to-day in the twentieth century.

The main road runs through the city of Hwochow from north to south, and many inns invite the traveller to rest, the red scrolls at the door assuring him that "From the four seas men all gather to this great hotel," and that the fame of its food is far-reaching.

Crossing this road from east to west is another important street where the official residence is situated. Here, most of the large shops are to be found and in the centre of the city is a fine tower, but all the smaller streets are alike, running between blank walls, from which access to as many as twelve courtyards may be through one small door. Numerous pigs walk unhindered up and down, acting as scavengers, and as such are not unneeded, for every one throws the refuse of the household out of the court door, caring nothing for the convenience of the public.

Parallel with the *Yamen* street is another important thoroughfare known as Prospect Hill. Here stands the largest and most important temple in the city, and almost next door to this, with the money given by his wife, Mr. Hsi secured small premises and announced that he was opening an opium refuge, and was willing to receive patients. Particulars as to rules and expenses were widely published, and in this place the first results of the love and self-sacrifice of Mrs. Hsi were seen.

A NEW VENTURE

"Love has a hem to its garment
That touches the very dust:
It can reach the stains of the streets and the lanes,
And because it can it must.

It dares not rest on the mountain;
It is bound to come to the vale;
For it cannot find its fulness of mind
Till it kindles the lives that fail."

George Matheson.

"The world had begun to stare, she half apprehended the fact, but she was in the presence of the irresistible. In the presence of the irresistible the conventional is a crazy structure, swept away with very little creaking of its timbers on the flood."
—George Meredith.

CHAPTER III

A NEW VENTURE

IN WHICH IS RECORDED THE APPOINTMENT OF
THE FIRST MISSIONARIES TO HWOCHOW

THE FIRST endeavour to bring the people of Hwochow within sound of the Gospel proved in every way encouraging. Numbers of men entered the Opium Refuge, and before long a nucleus of twenty were calling themselves Christians. The effort was, however, sterile so far as women were concerned, and Pastor Hsi knew the impossibility of establishing upon a solid basis a work which left untouched those who so largely controlled the home.

The power wielded by the woman in China is immense, for while she may be despised and, in her young days, even ill-treated, her day of power surely dawns, and woe betide the man who has to combat the determined will of mother or wife.

The question of providing women workers for Hwochow became a pressing one, and a visit from the Rev. Hudson Taylor was the occasion chosen by Pastor Hsi to bring before him the urgency of this claim.[1] His suggestion was that single women missionaries should be appointed who could give their time unreservedly to the teaching of women, and

---

1   It was on the occasion of this visit that Mr. Hsi was ordained pastor.

preaching. Mr. Taylor pointed out the difficulties and the misunderstanding which would make their lot far from easy, but these difficulties, Pastor and Mrs. Hsi felt, might be overcome, and willingly promised to give all the help which lay within their power. In any case, the claim of the women constituted a call to make a forward movement, and Mr. Taylor promised to give the matter serious consideration. By the end of that year, 1886, two Norwegian ladies had offered for the post.

Miss Jacobsen, an idealist, strong, capable, and critical, gave herself whole-heartedly to the work for which she had come. Enthusiastic and independent in thought and action, she soon acquired the spoken language to a remarkable degree, and with a praiseworthy tenacity she studied the classical works of the Chinese, and at the same time could vie with most of the women in all branches of their domestic activities. Her extraordinary ability is a byword to this day amongst the people who knew her.

She was accompanied by Miss Reuter, a lady of education and refinement, whose grace of manner and goodness of heart speedily endeared her to all with whom she came in contact. Varied as were the gifts and circumstances of the friends, they were one in desire and purpose. Their home was one small room, and here they dwelt and received all who came to them. They wore the Chinese dress, ate the Chinese food, and whether in their own home or in the villages where they preached, ever kept before them the one object of the salvation of souls.

As pioneer workers, enthusiasm sometimes overstepped discretion, and the violation of Chinese custom in such matters as the public playing of stringed instruments and open-air preaching to mixed congregations, led to misunderstanding, and even to the gathering around them of some whose presence was far from helpful.

Desire on the part of Miss Jacobsen to encourage in every way possible those who were already faced with persecution as they left idolatry, led to the preparation, each Sunday, of a simple meal which might be shared with any who walked long distances to attend services in the City Church, and who arrived weary and tired. Others, however, apart from the Christian family heard of this, and if matters of business brought them to the city, Sunday was considered an appropriate day to transact them, as thereby dinner might be obtained free. This naturally led to criticism on the part of the heathen, and many of the more independent and self-respecting people refrained from intercourse with a community of whom it could be said: "They believe for their food's sake." Acting upon the advice of Pastor Hsi, this practice was discontinued, the missionaries themselves willingly taking no food from morning until evening, that all might fare alike. It could but be evident to all concerned that the mistakes were those of love and enthusiasm, and such qualities do much to counteract any harm that might arise from unwise methods of expression. In every land, the world might well see more of the love that defies criticism, and forgets its own interests in whole-hearted devotion.

Bliss Reuter felt the importance of at once reaching the children, and opened a small school for the daughters of Christians. Three little girls were committed to her care, and these she faithfully taught, not despising the day of small things.

She, with Bliss Jacobsen, travelled from village to village with the evangelist Cheng Hsiu-chi, and preached the Gospel of Jesus Christ. Cheng was a native of Hwochow, and had,

> SCRIPTURE TESTIMONY
>
> *Counted worthy of suffering disgrace for the Name*
>
> ACTS 5:41

at Pastor Hsi's request, made ready the house for the missionaries when they came. As a young man he had wandered far in the paths of sin, and his mother, eager for his reformation, had spent no mean sum of money upon incense with which to seek the favour of the gods on his behalf. Seeing her devotion, his heart was touched, and he considered seeking refuge in a Buddhist monastery from the "fire of passion, hatred, and ignorance always burning in his heart." With this in view, he took counsel of a friend who had harboured similar ideals. This man had lately been a patient in the Refuge, where he had learnt of a stronger power to break the bonds of sin than fasting, penance, and self-discipline. With him Mr. Cheng attended a meeting of Christians where, meeting with Christ, he became a disciple. He returned home to face bitter persecution for refusing to pay the temple taxes; it was understood that no robbery of his crops, or ill-treatment of his person, would be punished by the village elders. He had finally no option but to leave his home and seek refuge elsewhere, rejoicing that he was counted worthy to suffer "for the Name's sake."

He then helped Pastor Hsi in the Hwochow Refuge, and later took charge of the same work in new and hitherto untouched districts, returning from time to time to his own city.

> **SCRIPTURE TESTIMONY**
>
> *There are no ethnic distinctions in Christ*
>
> GALATIANS 3:28

A strong admiration for Miss Jacobsen and her whole-hearted devotion awoke a consciousness that this feeling was not entirely on his side, and gradually, but surely, the difference of race and outlook was obliterated in the love which revealed to each the other's secret.

Those to whom Miss Jacobsen in honour bound confided her purpose, did all in their power to prevent what it seemed might prove to be a catastrophe to the work. She was asked to leave Hwochow, and was sent to another province. Some years passed, but nothing could change the determination which saw in this union a possible wider sphere of usefulness and understanding of the people she had come to love; moreover, the mysterious something which caused her to know that "one man loved the pilgrim soul" in her, could not be ignored. To her trusted friend Pastor Hsi, however, she did turn for advice, and while many fellow-workers found it hard to express their indignation and regret, he, with a clearness of outlook only possible where there is absence of prejudice, told her that while he could not regard it as a sin for a Christian man and woman of different races to marry, he felt convinced that the time had not come for such unions to be desirable.

As is usual in such cases where inclination runs contrary to the advice given, the latter was ignored, and in the year 1898 Cheng Hsiu-chi and Anna Jacobsen became man and wife. Painful as must have been the attitude of Westerners to Mrs. Cheng, a greater trial awaited her when she came to realise that the Chinese, both Christian and heathen, regarded her action with disapproval, and adopted so unappreciative an attitude both towards her husband and herself, that she found only critical antagonism where she had looked for sympathetic understanding. Mr. Cheng proved himself worthy in all ways of the confidence she had placed in him, and by self-sacrificing toil he, both before and after his wife's death, faithfully served the Lord to Whom he had yielded his life. In the year 1915 he too passed to his reward.

Miss Reuter had some time previously married Mr. Stanley Smith; young workers who had joined Miss Jacobsen for short periods had been moved to other places, and when fresh appointments were made it was a time of great difficulty. It was not easy to replace those whose absolute devotion had won the love of the people amongst whom they lived; and while Miss Jacobsen's action necessitated her withdrawal from the staff of the China Inland Mission, and made further residence in Hwochow impossible for her, they could not forget that she was the first missionary who had come to them, and that they were losing with her the man who had been a help to so many of them in their early Christian life.

THE CONTINUATION OF THE STORY

"Death is short, and life is long;
Satan is strong, and Christ more strong.
At His Word, Who hath led us hither,
The Red Sea must part hither and thither.
At His Word Who goes before us too,
Jordan must cleave to let us through."

C. Rossetti.

"On the other side of the River was also a meadow, curiously beautified with lilies, and it was green all the year round."—
Pilgrim's Progress.

CHAPTER IV

THE CONTINUATION OF THE STORY

BEING A RECORD OF SOME WHO WERE COUNTED WORTHY TO SUFFER FOR CHRIST'S SAKE, AND OF MRS. HSI'S EXPERIENCES IN THE BOXER OUTBREAK

CHANGES IN the staff at Taiyüanfu released for the oversight of mission work in Hwochow, Jane Stevens and Mildred Clarke. They might well shrink from the task facing them. Work in the provincial capital had been of so totally different an order, and life in a large community of foreigners had limited their sphere to the oversight of a small school for girls, and the instruction of women inquirers.

None had felt more strongly the seriousness of the step taken by Miss Jacobsen, and they came to Hwochow with the determination that all should early understand the impossibility of intercourse outside the most rigid observance of etiquette, Chinese and Western. Feeling strongly that such an attitude on their part would be the most helpful factor in the gathering around them of better-class women, they faithfully carried it into practice. Men who were connected with the Church were received by them only under the most formal restrictions. Finding it impossible to eat Chinese food, a simple, but foreign manage, took the place of the hitherto free-and-easy conditions.

It was a severe test for Chinese and foreigners alike; desire for renewal of the former conditions of intimacy met with no encouragement from those who could not but constantly bear the past in mind, and who felt that, for the highest interests of the work, a new relationship must be established. This attitude was naturally regarded as aloofness, and was galling to those whose love had been set on the young missionaries fresh from Norway, with all the enthusiasm of youth, to whom they themselves had taught the language and who belonged to them as others could not.

Miss Clarke gave her time to the Girls' School, the pupils of which now numbered nearly twenty, and those who followed her have reaped where she sowed. Often sad and weary she plodded on, but God in His time gave the increase. Aliss Stevens, to the limit of her strength, and often beyond it, faithfully worked in the city and villages, suffering much which to her was intense hardship, and feeling keenly the isolation and lack of confidence amongst the people who misunderstood the course of action deliberately adopted. Thus, while bringing heartache to themselves, these missionaries were enabled to make easy the way to all who followed them.

SCRIPTURE TESTIMONY
Killed for the sake of Christ
MATTHEW 16:24 · ACTS 7:58-60 · ACTS 12:1-5

The year 1900 dawned. In the month of June the ladies closed school and gladly accepted an invitation from friends in their old station to visit them. To Taiyüanfu they went, and after many anxious days spent with the missionaries gathered there they, in obedience to the Governor's command, helpless to disobey, even though they suspected his treacherous promises of protection, moved to a house near his *Yamen*.[1]

"Arrived at the house chosen for them, they made themselves as comfortable as possible for the night; and the next morning (Sunday, July 8) were able to examine their surroundings. They found that for their whole number (twenty- six, including children) there were only two comparatively small courts, the two inner courts being already occupied by the Roman Catholics. . . . When the fateful day (Monday, July 9) dawned, the

---

1   *Yamen* = law courts or Mansion House.

foreigners evidently had no inkling as to what was to happen. Just before noon the sub-prefect called and took a list of all who were in the house, both foreigners and Chinese, saying it was by order of the Governor. . . As was ascertained just a year later, when other Protestant missionaries returned to the province, the Governor had determined that on that day he would kill all the foreigners in Taiyüanfu. He evidently only took a few of the officials into his confidence, and one at least—the Tao Tai— strenuously opposed the course he was about to pursue, but unfortunately without result.

"It must have been about two o'clock in the afternoon when he ordered a number of officers, with their soldiers, to accompany him, and mounting his own horse, led the way. He made as though he would go out of the city by the North Gate, but before reaching that point, he suddenly wheeled round and went to the house where the missionaries were confined. He there ordered their immediate arrest, and they appear to have made no resistance—as, indeed, it would have been useless. All who were found within the compound (Protestants and Roman Catholics) were seized; and it so happened there were several Chinese there on business. . . . No excuse was listened to, and all were marched off to the Governor's *Yamen* between files of soldiers, where they were taken into the courtyard adjoining the street and surrounded by soldiers—not Boxers.

"As to what really occurred, the whole truth will probably never be known, but from inquiries made on the spot, it seems certain that the Governor did not assault any with his own hand; but, having asked the missionaries where they came from, and being answered, 'From England,' and 'From France,' just gave the order, 'Sha' (kill) to the soldiers, who answered with a shout and immediately fell upon their defenceless victims, killing them indiscriminately."[1]

The Church in Hwochow, Chaoeheng, and Fensi had a marvellous escape. The Boxers, practising their mystic rites, overran the district. Whole families fled to the mountains, and no one was safe from robbery and violence. The mandarin of Chaoeheng, fearful lest massacres should take place in the county under his jurisdiction and desiring at any cost to

---

1   From *Fire and Sword in Shansi*, by Dr. E. H. Edwards.

keep the peace, called together some of the leading gentry and asked for advice as to the problem facing them. "I know," said he, "that calling upon the Christians to recant will be useless, but can we not issue tickets to them upon which are the very words they use in entering the Church, 'I promise to repent?' There should be no difficulty in getting them to take these, for it will mean to them what they themselves preach, while to the anti-Christian fanatic it will be sufficiently satisfactory."

Orders were accordingly issued that all Christians were to receive this official paper whereby their safety would be ensured. Large numbers in the Church regarded the mandarin's action as the overruling of Providence on their behalf, and accepted tickets which involved no verbal recantation of their faith. Others, amongst whom was Mrs. Hsi (now a widow), with more sensitive spiritual perceptions, refused to take advantage of even the semblance of a subterfuge.

The Chaocheng mandarin, surrounded by his bodyguard, went outside the city gates to the place where the Boxers were practising their rites with the intention of burning incense in their presence, by which act he would acknowledge them as invulnerable and holy men. At the critical moment, however, one of them was said to have made a move as if to attack the official, who instantly called upon his bodyguard to seize the men, exclaiming: "These are insurgents, and no holy men; bind them, they are prisoners." As such they entered the city, and Boxerism never spread in the district. Thus did the Hand of God protect the hundreds of men and women who in these three counties were called by His Name, and while in many places few escaped the sword, the numerically largest Church in the province of Shansi was spared.

Mrs. Hsi was in Chaocheng seeking to help the women in their troubles, when news reached her that her brother-in-law, Elder Si, was stabbed by one of the local Boxers. Rumours followed rapidly, and she heard that her mother-in-law was in serious danger. She hastened to her home, and found matters worse than she had feared. There was no place in which to live, the house was destroyed, her clothes were stolen, and had it not been for the thoughtfulness of one missionary who, in the midst of personal danger, found time to buy and send to her some garments and bedcovering, she would have been in a sad plight. Her old mother could not walk, so badly had she been beaten by the robbers, and terrified, the two women crept to the fields and hid themselves. When night fell they returned to shelter and to get a little food, crawling out to their hiding-place before the cock crew each morning. Terror was upon the whole populace. The official had not been successful here, as in Chaocheng, in dealing with the movement, and the party of missionaries who had for some time been gathered in Pingyangfu were openly attacked and robbed by Boxer bands as they left the city under official escort.

In loneliness and peril Mrs. Hsi and her aged mother cried to God, as the anxious, weary days passed by. The missionaries were gone, very many killed, others in hiding, and some, after perils and sufferings unspeakable, had reached Hankow. After some months came the additional sorrow of the death of her brother-in-law, Elder Si, who had managed for her all matters in which she required help.

Gradually the storm blew over, but those who passed through that period can never forget it. For Christ's sake they had suffered, and they could not again be as before. The Church in Shansi "had a new and powerful weapon" in her hands, "the power of her sufferings."

A few months later, as soon as passports were available, the missionaries were back at their posts. There was much to tell and to hear, as old friends met and were able to recount all the wonderful deliverances of the past year. But how many vacant places there were! How could they be filled? Ripe experience and Christlike sympathy were needed to deal with the new situation.

Some had, under pressure, in a weak moment, recanted; others had resisted this temptation, but fallen over the more subtle question of indemnity for property destroyed. The situation, moreover, was changed; foreigner and Christian alike were now in the ascendancy. Compensation for life and property was granted, and though the members of the China Inland Mission declined to accept this, their action was made the occasion of a laudatory proclamation which called upon the people to note and imitate such an exemplification of self-forgetting goodness.

In the providence of God the lives of a few missionaries had been spared to return, and with the benefit of their experience, to help new workers to an understanding of a situation which, mishandled, would inevitably lead to disastrous consequences.

Nothing could give Mrs. Hsi greater pleasure than to hear from her friend, Miss French, that Hwochow was to be her future centre. I, as a new worker, was to accompany her, and together we reached the city which was to be henceforth our home.

The reception given by the very few Christians who gathered to meet us, was both cordial and critical. Miss French was welcome as being one whose reputation had long ago reached them, who had already paid several visits to the station, and whose Chinese, they soon remarked, was "as good as Miss Jacobsen's!" Of me they knew nothing, and I had to meet the gaze of many eyes and listen to the remark, before I opened my mouth to speak, that it was impossible to understand my words. I had only one asset, and that was the fact that this being my first station I should belong to them, and when the day dawned that would release my stammering tongue, the honour of having taught and trained me would be theirs!

LIFE IN THE VILLAGES

"Great things are done when men and mountains meet;
These are not done by jostling in the street."

William Blake.

"Arrived there, the little house they fill,
No look for entertainment where none was;
Rest is their feast, and all things at their will;
The noblest mind the best contentment has."

William Spenser.

CHAPTER V

LIFE IN THE VILLAGES

AN INTRODUCTION TO CHINESE HOME LIFE

THE HOUSE at Hwochow, which we were to inhabit, was still in the hands of workmen. We therefore decided to delay the unpacking of our boxes, and to spend several months in visiting the homes of the Christians throughout the four counties for which we were then responsible. Our travelling paraphernalia was simple, luggage being limited to the amount that a small donkey could carry in addition to a rider. Clothes and books were tied up in large square handkerchiefs and distributed as evenly as possible, along with a folded, wadded quilt in a long bed-bag which, thrown over the donkey's saddle, reached nearly to the ground on either side. On the early morning of the day decided on for our departure, two donkeys thus laden stood at our gate. On to one of them I was hoisted, and took my first lesson in how to sit happily, perched high on the voluminous luggage with neither reins for my hands nor stirrups for my feet, for sometimes as long as twelve hours' travelling with but a short break for food and rest at midday. From village to village we wandered, received everywhere with cordial hospitality, pressed to extend our visit, and followed on our departure by the reiterated cry: "Come again, come again, come again soon!"

All was fresh and delightful to me and brimful of interest, from the hour when I rode through the city gate, passed the great tanks of lotus bloom to the edge of the swift, shallow river, where my servant stripped off his shoes and socks to lead my donkey knee-deep over the ford.

By narrow roads we travelled where the tall grain stood like a wall on either side, ripening in the fierce sunshine which bathed the landscape in a dazzling glare. Through occasional villages we rode, where the women called to each other to hurry and see the strange sight, and groups of naked and semi-naked children commented freely on the appearance of the "foreign devils."

A few miles farther and the first stage was reached—a deep court-yard backing the hillside, from which had been hollowed a row of caves according to the economical method of the country. Scarcely any bricks are required for such building, and the deep, lofty, arched room affords the warmest shelter in our bitter Shansi winter cold, as it does the coolest refuge from the burning summer heat.

"Come again, come again soon," and we were off again, refreshed by a delicious, beautifully cooked meal, and our hearts warmed by the evident pleasure which our visit had given and the cordial hospitality which had sought to let us know how welcome we were. And now we left the fertile plain and well-watered land which lay all along the river-bed to climb steep, stony roads, and follow narrow footpaths, where the difficulty of its broad load made my donkey step gingerly as near to the chasm's edge as she could secure a foothold, and I dug my knees into the soft bed-bag and longed for something on which I could get a grip. How pleasant and easy such journeying became before the end of that autumn's wandering, and how familiar the life of the village homes. Almost day by day the confused sounds took form to my unaccustomed ears, and I was soon able to differentiate quite clearly between the two inevitable questions, "How old are you?" and "How many brothers and sisters have you?" I ceased to cover myself with confusion, by answering that my brothers and sisters numbered twenty- three, and that my age was six—though now that the days of helpless shame are passed, I would not not have made these mistakes, so keen is the enjoyment still felt when some one repeats the old joke, and all laugh merrily at the recollection.

Happy, irresponsible days, in which I learned to know and love the Chinese. I saw them now to best advantage, simple, patriarchal, industrious and thrifty, extraordinarily resourceful, and independent of all that their own fields and farm do not supply. I saw the women's activities, and how they picked the cotton in the fields, spun and carded it, then wove it into strong cloth on the loom made for them by their own husbands; how they dyed the cloth with indigo of their own growing, and finally converted it into the garments, and even the shoes and socks, worn by the whole family. I saw how those same garments were wadded with a layer of cotton-wool as the cold season approached, and behold, the whole family was made proof against the severe onslaughts of the keenest frosts and bitterest winds. I saw how a measure of wheaten or maize flour, a vessel of water, and a few vegetables dug from the field were daily converted into the three meals on which young and old alike thrived, the men showing a muscular development and endurance and an agility unequalled by anything I had met in other countries. I learned to recognise their simple, unexpressed joys, and to realise the deep tragedies which lay beneath the surface of their laborious lives.

I was in the midst of the province which—in the very year when I was born—had been swept by the horrors of a famine and pestilence which left whole villages with no other survivor than perhaps two or three wailing children, feeding on garbage torn from the grasp of the dead hand.

My servant remembered the time well. His whole family had been wiped out, and he had escaped as by a miracle. "In those days, dogs ate dogs and men ate men," was the refrain of his tale, only too literally and absolutely true, for no man dared to venture on the lonely path leading from one village to another, knowing that the likelihood was that murderers lay in wait, and that a few picked bones alone would tell the tale even if, satiated with horrors to the point of indifference, any one cared to inquire of it.

When I expressed surprise at the many rows of caves allowed to fall into utter ruin, and the traces of whole villages now returned to waste land: "Famine year," he would briefly answer, "dogs ate dogs and men ate men."

I learned, too, why it was that no merry groups of children wandered away from the village, even now when no evil-doers lay in wait, upon some game or exploring adventure. I first discovered the reason of this through meeting a woman whose face was scarred and mutilated so as to bear small likeness to the human, and on inquiry I was informed that, as a little girl, she had strayed away from home and been attacked by a wolf; men had rushed to her rescue, but her face, which is generally the part first attacked, was torn beyond recognition. I then learned what a common thing it is for wild beasts, wolves or leopards, to come down from the hills, and steal children even as they play around the courtyard grinding-stone. I could not be surprised at the intense anxiety of a woman whose son was half an hour late returning from an errand, when I heard that her eldest child had strayed off one day, and never been seen again. I was told of yet another woman who, nursing her baby in the cave, saw a leopard spring on her eldest child in the courtyard. Frantic, she left the baby to raise the alarm, and when she returned bearing the little mangled body' in her arms, she found that the wild beast's mate had noted her absence and carried the baby off to its lair.

I also heard, and found myself compelled to believe, things which I should have dismissed with an incredulous smile some few months earlier.

It was now that I found myself brought face to face with the strange phenomenon of demon possession. There is so much to be said on this interesting topic, that it will require a chapter under its own heading to note even a portion of what has come under my personal notice. For the first time I heard, often in the midnight stillness, the high-pitched voice, intoning the magic incantations whereby some young woman yielded herself to be the medium of communication between the spirit and the material, the wild chant sometimes dying away in the distance, as she led a group of inquirers over wild mountain paths in obedience to the directions of her control.

> **SCRIPTURE TESTIMONY**
>
> *Christians are generous and hospitable*
>
> ACTS 16:14-15 · ROMANS 12:13 · I
> TIMOTHY 3:2 · HEBREWS 13:2

A few weeks were spent in the home of an elder of the Church, Giang by name, as from this centre it was easy to make daily itinerations in the neighbourhood. What a welcome we received there! The deep cave set apart for our use was decorated with flowers, everything was clean and comfortable, and we were made to feel "at home." Being guests in the house, our meals were always served separately, but we liked to take our bowls into the courtyard and enjoy the family life. We were able to consult with our host concerning many whom we had visited during the day, and discuss our plans for the morrow.

As the daylight faded we joined in prayer and praise, and listened to much that was of interest to us as the Elder told of early years spent in dissipation, opium smoking, and gambling; of his conversion through Pastor Hsi, and of first efforts to preach the Gospel. Meanwhile, the shepherd folded his sheep, carefully counting them lest one should be missing, and the women prepared the millstones for grinding on the morrow.

I saw much illustrated that had been familiar to me from childhood in the Gospel stories, even to the midnight cry announcing the arrival of the bridal party to a neighbour's house. A little oil was added to our long-extinguished lamp, as, being first to hear the clanging of the cymbals, we hastened to the bridegroom's home to help arouse the drowsy guests.

We returned in due course to Hwochow, urged by our kind hostess to come again at any time. Such homes are resting-places to those who have left home for the Kingdom of God's sake, and are part of the literal fulfilment of the promise: "An hundredfold now in this time."

Nowhere are we more sure of a welcome than in some of these Chinese courts, and for the Church of Christ in the home of Elder Giang, I for one shall ever be thankful.

OUR RECEPTION AT HWOCHOW

"The Master said: At first, my way with men was to hear their words, and give them credit for their conduct. Now, my way is to hear their words, and look at their conduct."—*Confucian Analects*.

"The Master said: A man should say, I am not concerned that I have no place, I am concerned how I may fit myself for one. I am not concerned that I am not known, I seek to be worthy to be known."—*Confucian Analects*.

CHAPTER VI

OUR RECEPTION AT HWOCHOW

SHOWING THINGS AS THEY SOMETIMES ARE

IN SPITE of the valuable help given by study circles, training-colleges, and other means by which the candidate for the mission field is equipped for his work, I question if many are fully prepared, when they arrive at the station to which they have been appointed, to find themselves studied, summed up, and criticised by the people to whom they have come in the capacity of teachers, and from whom they unconsciously expected some measure of deference.

The Westerner, as such, has no prestige in the eyes of the Chinese, and though his wealth, education, and business capacity may command more or less respect, the deep-rooted feeling is a sense of the intrinsic superiority of the Middle Kingdom and its sons to the barbaric subjects of a vague territory known as the "Kingdom without"— that is, without the pale of the ancient civilisation. By grace, the Christian will welcome you as a fellow-subject of the Kingdom of God, but on this ground only, and on no preconceived assumption of your superiority, will you be accepted.

The fact that you have come several thousands of miles in order to preach the Gospel, is not sufficient to place you unquestionably on a pedestal. By temperament you are either impetuous or slow, easy-going or exacting, courteous or brusque, and you will prove to be by nature more or less reasonable or unreasonable when the Chinaman seeks to make you understand *li,* an untranslatable word, which embodies the idea of the complete range of all that it is suitable that you should be and do, on every occasion.

Failure to readjust your mind to such conditions during the first years of your missionary life may prove an eventual fatal barrier to mutual sympathetic understanding, and the establishment of that barrier has been one of the difficulties which has not been much spoken of by those with whom you have conversed, though they have doubtless been keenly conscious of it themselves.

We returned to Hwochow. The house was ready for us, and so were the Church members. "New people," said some, "we are unaccustomed to each other; they do not understand our circumstances, and we do not know them."

"Why did they spend months in another district instead of coming at once to make themselves acquainted with us, our affairs, and our homes?"

"It is a case of clear neglect," said another. "I have been a Church member for fifteen years, and all the notice they have taken of me is to spend one paltry day in my home, whereas they were three whole days in the village of Peace and Harmony, where there are only heathen and not a Christian to receive them. "I," complained another, "have been unable to attend Church service for two weeks, and neither of them has been near, as yet, to inquire the cause of my absence."

"Well," chimed in an old gentleman, who by reason of his seniority in the Church carried a good deal of weight, "had our beloved teacher of former days been here, our homes would have been visited, and I will take the first opportunity of telling them my mind on the subject."

The close of the following Sunday morning service found us sad enough. The congregation numbered thirty, and while some were loyally ready to help, there was a section of malcontents who since the early days had been a source of difficulty to Pastor Hsi and his friends, and from whom, in the light of past knowledge, Miss French knew that trouble would come.

The first indication of the brewing storm was the entrance to our guest-room of an aged Church member who, by reason of his rank as military mandarin, was one of the glories of the Hwochow Church. Vigorous and stalwart, his seventy years sat lightly on him, his bearing and the play of his facial muscles affording proof of the brilliancy with which he had passed the necessary examinations for the obtaining of his degree. Unlike the civil mandarin, whose examinations require such arduous study of classical writings, the military honour was conferred as a reward for physical prowess. The competitor was required to exhibit great skill in archery, shooting at the target from the back of a galloping horse, and to lift stones of immense weight; meanwhile throwing the body into such postures as, coupled with a terrifying expression of the countenance and accompanied by blood-curdling yells, would strike such terror into the heart of the opponent that he would flee without striking a blow.

After such training he had little to fear, and felt, no doubt, that a few moments' interview would be sufficient to reduce two young women to reason, and place matters on a more satisfactory basis.

When the old gentleman entered, we invited him to the seat of honour, ourselves taking chairs at the lower side of the table. He asked for an explanation. Had he been informed correctly that we had been appointed to carry on the work in Hwochow? "Yes," we replied, "that is the case, and also to help the women in the counties of Chaocheng, Hungtung, and Fensi, until such time as lady workers shall be in residence there; moreover, our schools are to be for the women and girls of these counties as well as Hwochow."

This item of information fell as a severe blow. Hwochow is a curious district, its natives physically and mentally being of a totally different type to all around, in all relationships with whom there exists mutual distrust and suspicion. It was odious to men and women of this exclusive type to hear that the foreigner, in coming, viewed the nurturing of a small band of discontents as of very secondary importance to the opportunity of spreading the news of the Gospel far and wide amongst the heathen. It was at this point of the conversation that the first traces of that terror-striking expression began to flit across his features, and his eyebrows gathered themselves into a most terrifying bunch. "Are you aware that I have been a Christian for twelve years, and that I am known far and wide by Chinese and foreigners alike?" "I am fully aware of it," said Miss French, and might have added, "known and dreaded of all men."

"Should not the missionaries' conduct be regulated in accordance with the command, 'Seek the lost until it be found'?" "It should," acquiesced Miss French. "Then are you aware that during the past three months we have been as sheep without a shepherd, left a prey to wolves, with no one to care for us, our homes have been unvisited, and members who have absented themselves from Church service have had no inquiries made as to the cause of their non-appearance?"

"Did you say *twelve* years a Church member?" inquired Miss French. "Nearly thirteen," he replied. "Then no longer a babe in Christ, but yourself able to seek the lost, and to come to our assistance as we take up the responsibilities of our new work. We have come here," she added, "for the people who need us, whether Chaoeheng or Hwochow."

"Then go to Chaoeheng and leave us alone; *our* missionaries must shepherd *our* Church." At this point wrath overcame him, and throwing himself into the classical position of the Chinese brave, "A couple of youngsters," he yelled, "untaught in the wisdom of Confucius." With these words he flung himself out of the room. His spirit was too much perturbed to call to mind the wisdom of the sage, "In archery we have something like the way of the superior man. When the archer misses the centre of the target, he turns round and seeks for the cause of his failure in himself."

The loud clanging of a gong was shortly heard, and the tones of a well-known voice alternately carolling forth a familiar hymn 'with a recital of the wrongs needing redress.

> "The Gospel way is the best of all, hark! I loud proclaim the same."
> (Loud beating of the gong.)
> "Call that love! I vow to report them at headquarters!"
> "Heaven's joy bestowed on earth, saves poor sinners and sets them free."

(Again the gong.)

"Much they care for our souls! Let them go to Chaocheng!"

The sounds gradually ceased, as those who were truly grieved that we should be thus insulted pacified the old gentleman, begging him to have a care for his aged body, and refresh it with food and rest.

Miss French's mind was made up. "We shall soon make another tour of villages outside this district," she said, "and it shall be a long one. These old members have stood in the way long enough. New converts will join themselves to the Church; if they be welcomed, all the better, if not, the old ones must go; we can allow them to hinder no longer."

Miss French's method was fully justified, for when they saw new adherents keen with the flush of first love and enthusiasm they, with very few exceptions, awakened more fully to their responsibilities.

Time heals many wounds, and when we returned from England our old friend, the military mandarin, came in full official dress to welcome us.

"Good to have you back," he said; "we are accustomed to each other, and you know how to manage this place!"

A PORTRAIT GALLERY

"We must be as courteous to a man as we are to a picture, which we are willing to give the advantage of a good light."—Emerson.

"He asked them to come with Him, and they came; and Jesus did not begin by raising questions in their minds as to whether they were worthy to come. It was the purpose of Jesus to make them worthy to stay. Now the Church of Christ ought to be as hospitable as Christ was. I do not see for what other purpose she exists. And the Church ought to be as confident and believing as Christ was, that many a one whom it may be was unworthy to enter has at length become worthy to remain." —Dr. John Hutton.

CHAPTER VII

A PORTRAIT GALLERY

WHEREIN THE READER IS INTRODUCED TO
SOME OF OUR FELLOW WORKERS

I N MEETING the members of an infant and unsophisticated Church, it is delightful to observe the directness of their spiritual characteristics, unfettered by the artificiality which grows up with theological phraseology and the adoption of sectarian conventionalities.

So strongly individualistic a band of men met us at Hwochow, that Christian himself on his Heavenward journey encountered, I think, no more varied a company, nor more striking, in the various ways in which Christ had met them and called them to discipleship, and turned their strongly- marked characteristics into the way of His service.

Evangelist, Fu by name, keen and even fierce in his determination to compel men to hear the truth concerning the City of Destruction and the burden of sin which rests upon them, would go from place to place with a bundle of books, preaching and warning sinners "to flee from the wrath to come." He asked no remuneration from the Church or foreigner for the time he gave, but realising that necessity was laid upon him, he pointed men to the Saviour. His best work was done alone for he was easily offended, but, true and straight, he ruled his house in the fear of the Lord.

His conversion was characteristic of the man. Having business to transact in the small city of Great Peace, he found that large crowds had gathered to listen to a man proclaiming strange doctrines. Every one knew why Pastor Hsi, for it was he, had come that day to the city. A family had professed their willingness to destroy idols, and asked him to be present on the occasion. When the Pastor arrived, however, the man had changed his mind, and fear of consequences had proved too much for him. Nothing could hinder the Pastor from preaching the Good News, and he made much of this opportunity. When he had finished speaking, Mr. Fu went to him and asked him what was this new doctrine, and Mr. Hsi told him the story of the Garden of Eden, and the Fall of man.

"In Adam all have sinned, and in Christ all can be forgiven." It was a strange story, and yet as Fu listened he felt it was true, and as he took the long, lonely walk over the mountains to his home, he meditated much upon it. He had not as yet seen the wicket-gate, but he had seen the direction in which it lay, and a subconscious desire was in his heart to know more.

SCRIPTURE TESTIMONY
Signs and wonders draw attention to Gospel message
JOHN 4:28-29 · ACTS 8:5-8

Home affairs claimed his attention, and he had no time to give to the further investigation of new religions; and yet the seed which had been sown was gradually germinating, so that when after a few months he found himself again near Great Peace, in a small place where was an opium refuge, Mr. Fu went in to see the man who was in charge. Although he had never smoked opium himself, Mr. Fu was on this occasion in possession of some of the crude drug, and was on his way to the hills to sell it, and hoped by the transaction to profit considerably. The Refuge-keeper, seeing he was interested, asked him to share his evening meal, and when he found out the errand on which his guest was bent, he told him to sell the opium he had and avoid any further dealings with so deadly a poison. Mr. Fu was deeply touched by the kindness of this man. "I have no claim upon him, and yet he treated me as a brother," was his reflection. From that day Mr. Fu never sold opium again.

He started on his homeward journey, and once more as he walked the lonely roads he was conscious of the constraining presence of One who has so often met with men as they travel, walking through the fields, and inviting them to leave all and follow Him. Thus untrammelled by the words and requirements of men, Mr. Fu met with his rod; but still questioning, he reached home to find that his wife was dangerously ill. He went at once to a neighbouring village to fetch a doctor, and found him unwilling to come until he had taken a dose of opium which was then due. Finding that all persuasion was useless, Mr. Fu suddenly decided to go to Hwochow and see if the foreign missionaries, or the Opium Refuge - keeper there, had any medicine. He walked the twelve miles, and was directed to the missionaries' house. The decision to go to Hwochow was made suddenly, not so the resolution to enter the open door of the house. Perhaps he had been wrong after all! It was serious to so openly come in contact with foreigners! It might be that the stories he had heard of their magical powers were correct! And yet his heart had borne him witness, in that lonely walk, that what he heard in Great Peace was true.

After walking up and down for some time, unconscious that Goodwill was watching him from within, he heard some one call and ask him to come in. The call came at the right moment and he entered, knowing as he did so that a definite step was being taken and life would never be for him the same again.

"My wife is ill, and I have come to ask for medicine," he said. After some talk he was taken to see Miss Jacobsen, who told him that God could, and would, heal sickness in answer to prayer. She and the evangelist prayed with him, gave him medicine, some books; and made him promise to come again. He left them, saying that he would do so. Again the long, lonely walk had to be faced, and Beelzebub gave orders that arrows should be shot at him, and all manner of doubts took possession of his soul. "I must go again, for I have given my word," he reflected. "What folly!" and then again the words which he could not doubt reasserted themselves, and he considered, yielded, and believed.

As he entered his courtyard, he saw his wife grinding corn! "I am well," she said. "And I," he said, "have believed in Jesus." To his surprise, not one word of anger escaped her lips. "I am glad," was her only comment.

There was no time to be lost; if he delayed, others might hinder him, and before his evening meal he tore down the idols, and together husband and wife prayed to God.

Fu was the youngest of four brothers, and the three other families were not of the same mind; he was unceasing in his efforts to bring them to the Saviour, but at the Chinese New Year festival they, as custom required, burnt incense to the idols.

Serious illness seized upon various members of all three families, and their lives were in danger. Fu, seeing his opportunity, offered to go to the city and ask the evangelist to come and pray for them, and to this they consented. When Mr. Fu returned, he was accompanied by Mr. Cheng, and in response to his exhortations their idols were destroyed and the three brothers professed their willingness to become disciples. That place has been signally blessed of God. All have given liberally of their substance to the work of the Lord, and they have now their own church, a cave cut from the *loess* cliffs by their own hands, where Sunday by Sunday men and women gather from the neighbouring villages to hear the word of God, and many have been added to the Church as a result.

*   *   *   *   *   *   *   *

SCRIPTURE TESTIMONY
Believers are the aroma of Christ to those around them
2 CORINTHIANS 2:14-16

Mr. Ging, little of stature, so short-sighted as to be almost blind, had recently been a patient in the Opium Refuge. A scholar of note, holding a high degree, we first knew him when he was about forty years of age, and the only Christian in his village. He was more than any Chinaman I have met impregnated with the teachings of Confucius; and filial piety was for him no mere doctrine of words, but a ruling factor in his life.

Shortly before the time of which I write, he had, one day, given some cause of offence to his aged mother, in consequence of which she commanded that, in recognition of his fault, he should kneel on the ground before her until such time as she should see fit to excuse him.

For half a day she kept him in that position, and he knelt quietly, giving to all an example and illustration of the sacred duty of son to parent as taught in the Chinese Classics, and as understood by those who earnestly follow their teachings.

By virtue of his learning and position, no matter of importance would be settled in the village without him, and he enjoyed great respect as a teacher of the young, notwithstanding the fact that he was handicapped in his work as schoolmaster by reason of his defective eyesight, the boys taking full advantage of his disability and failing to appreciate as they should the virtue of the "Princely Man" of whom they read so much in their classical studies, and of whom they daily witnessed so striking an example.

For some of these pupils of his, examination day dawned, and the results were disastrous. The consequences of much undetected mischief were now made clear in the light of day, and the indignant examining missionary called upon Mr. Ging to aid in devising a punishment adequate to the circumstances. "Is it by extra imposed work, or by the public disgrace of the rod, that their misdeeds will be made most heinous in their own eyes?" he was asked, the remarks being accompanied by a look which could not fail to assure the trembling band of offenders that the method of Solomon met with unqualified approval. "I think," replied Mr. Ging, "that the case does not call so much for punishment as for exercise of greater patience on our side!!!" This answer was to the unbounded delight of the scholars, and discomfiture of the missionary.

It was in his own village and home that he shone. Before many years had passed, the people who were formerly unwilling to receive us had many of them become Christians. One of their number had lent his room, rent free for ten years, as a meeting-place for worship, and a good work had begun. If you spoke to them of the cause of this change, they would tell you of Mr. Ging and the force of his example, and how even his old mother had, before her death, renounced idolatry and asked for a Christian funeral.

What can I say of Mr. Lan? One is tempted to question, "How shall the superficial enter into the Kingdom of God?"

One of the aristocratic families, no longer enjoying the prosperity of former days, yet endeavouring to impress upon all its grandeur whilst inevitably sinking, gave us Mr. Lan.

Contact with Pastor Hsi had been the turning point in his life, and from the early days he gave himself assiduously to the study of the Bible. Few have more accurate knowledge of the Scripture than he, his addresses are well and carefully-prepared, and he has been the means under God of leading many men to a knowledge of the Saviour. His kind disposition and good-nature have given him many friends, but love of money and appearances have crippled his usefulness. Any Christian work he now does is independent of the missionaries, and he will sometimes be invited to the official's residence to help some one to leave the opium habit, he and his father before him having been doctors of no small repute. He is constantly in debt, and will often remain away from his home during the Chinese New Year when debts are settled, but when he does return, he enters the house with such perfect manners, and is attired in such gorgeous silk, that few would venture to mention anything so unpleasant as the settlement of a debt.

Easily led, he loves the glories of this present world and is fearful lest, by too great zeal, the rulers of Vanity Fair may regard him as a stranger and outcast. And yet, in his high moments, he finds himself longing for the things that abide, and his affections and desires are for the time being upon these, but as a morning cloud they pass. In other lands, where the line of demarcation is less clear, he might be considered a good Churchman, but neutral tints are rare here, and a man must clearly show on which side he stands Or he will get the benefit of neither.

He is ever faithfully served by his dependant and sycophant, Mr. Diao, who is a weak, physically decadent man who can neither offend by word nor deed the man from whom he has had so much, His manner is too servile to allow one to place much confidence in him, but he is a believer, and proves by many actions that he is truly following Christ. If only he could get free from the net of the rich man, and yet—what Church has not such members!

SCRIPTURE TESTIMONY
God will provide for our daily needs
MATTHEW 6:11

Mr. Tu, weak, good, always trusting the Heavenly Father to supply his needs, temporal and spiritual, and ever ready to bear witness that

He has done so, in spite of the fact that life's outlook is always grey! Very poor, he was the leader in his village by virtue of his sincerity. Is some aggressive movement proposed? "The time has not yet come," is his ever-ready answer. Do the crops seem to fail for lack of rain, and the farmers, anxious and worried, speak of the famine confronting them, and him? "Fear not, the Lord will provide," he will say, and though he may have to eat the coarsest flour, and little of that sometimes, he never doubts, and never rejoices!!

On the occasion of the marriage of his son, even a short time before the bride arrived, nothing was ready—he had so little—and all he said was: "We must wait and see how the Heavenly Father will provide." When the moment came every one was ready to help him, and he would be a discontent indeed who was dissatisfied with the result. Mr. Tu was full of praise to God for His goodness, and will quote the incident to those who may have doubts.

I have reflected much upon Mr. Tu and his ways, and I am reminded of the ravens, "who sow not nor gather into barns," and our Heavenly Father cares for them; and I come to the conclusion that to us is granted on rare occasions the privilege of being the medium by which our Father will prove His care to the weak, yet trustful souls. Good, faithful old Tu, he could teach many of us of the active, energetic temperament a lesson; for he will tell you, and truly, that he has no strength, yet he has never asked from man, and he has perfect confidence that the Good Shepherd will lead him safe to the journey's end.

WORK DEVELOPMENT

"No Church is fulfilling its responsibilities to God, or preparing itself for its best and most effective work, which does not regard itself in some respects as a great Training School for Christian workers."—Rev. A. Swift.

> "And He gave—
> Some indeed to be apostles,
> And some prophets,
> And some evangelists,
> And some shepherds and teachers,—
> With a view to the fitting of the saints
> For the work of ministering,
> For an upbuilding of the body of the Christ."
>   The Letter of Paul to the Ephesians.

CHAPTER VIII

WORK DEVELOPMENT

RELATING HOW WE SOUGHT TO ENCOMPASS THE WORK, AND THE WORK ENCOMPASSED US

THE EVENTS of 1900 resulted in an extraordinary quickening of interest amongst those who had a contact of some kind with Christianity. We very soon found ourselves quite overwhelmed by the many openings and opportunities which presented themselves on all sides. Hitherto untouched villages begged for a visit, idols were destroyed by those into whose homes we had never penetrated, leaders in the Church were begging us to devise some means by which the women might be taught, fathers were prepared for any sacrifice so that their daughters might be received as scholars.

For some time, at vast expenditure of strength, we attempted by travelling in different directions to spend, at any rate, one or two days in the various centres we were begged to visit. Each month we became more strongly impressed with the fact that the work of evangelisation was being carried on with tremendous aggressive force, not by us, but by the native Church, we being unable to even follow up the openings made by them.

Such a mass movement afforded an unparalleled opportunity, provided sufficient teaching were given to establish and build up in the faith those who believed; but if left to itself, this large numerical increase might prove a serious menace to the spiritual life of the Church. We had to seriously consider our ways. Should we contribute our small part to the widespread preaching of the Gospel and visiting of those who had already heard through the Chinese evangelising agencies, or should we leave to the Chinese Church the responsibility of propagating itself, reserving ourselves to "preparing saints for the work of ministering"?

Chinese Christians going from place to place spread the Good Tidings more effectually than we could hope to do, and where such conditions exist, it is surely an indication that the people of the land should hear the Gospel first from the lips of their own countrymen. Moreover, the Government was seriously considering the establishment of girls' schools, and we had to decide as to whether the work amongst the young should be an unimportant branch of our scheme of missionary activities, or whether our schools should be established with the object of becoming training-centres for Christian helpers.

We were faced with this fact: unless we trained some Christian teachers, the education of the young would be in the hands of heathen; no small matter when the exalted position of the teacher in China is borne in mind; and the, if possible, more urgent fact, that unless we seriously prepared some Chinese missionaries we should go from year to year, decade to decade, with no trained Chinese staff. The material was there, and the Chinese Church was supplying young men and women, earnest devoted servants of Jesus Christ, who, given the training and granted the blessing of God, could do a work which it would be impossible for the most earnest Westerner to accomplish. Chinese of the Chinese, with neither linguistic nor climatic difficulties, understanding the minds of the most subtle of people, they enter their work with a flying leap which we may envy, but cannot attain. The Holy Spirit will deal with them as He does with us, and recognising them as fellow-workers together with God, we shall cease to hinder them by perpetual criticism and doubt. Faults they will have, as we, and while of a different order, who shall say that these failings make them in God's sight more unfit for the work of preaching the Gospel than ours have made us?

We therefore accepted the form of ministry which pressed with strongest necessity on us, and from the free and irresponsible life of the itinerant missionary, accepted the calling of teachers, and allowed ourselves to be tied to the numberless claims and responsibilities of institutional life. In addition to the girls' school, a plan was formed whereby we agreed to accept married women for terms of varying length— twenty to thirty days—as far as possible classifying them according to ability and previous knowledge. The teaching was graded from the first elements of Christian doctrine to fairly advanced New Testament classes. From amongst the first groups of women who came to us, it was evident that some were capable of receiving a far more advanced training, and the zeal they exhibited in teaching the little they knew on their return home, promised well for future usefulness. Two small rooms in our own living-court supplied the only accommodation for these station classes, and as each group scattered it was almost immediately replaced by other eager inquirers.

A small inner court containing two good rooms was set apart for the use of the girls' school. Every term brought an increase in the numbers, and it was soon evident that more

SCRIPTURE TESTIMONY
God's work will not lack God's supply
PHILIPPIANS 4:19

suitable accommodation was essential if we were to meet the growing need. Though we knew it not, the necessary provision was already made. We sat together one evening in a shady spot adjoining our premises, sharing our home letters; we opened one to find it contained a cheque from a friend who could know nothing of our need, marked: "For use in any necessary buildings." The very spot on which we sat, later on proved to be the site of the John Holt Skinner Memorial Court in the new school buildings. By the next term Chinese rooms, providing for the accommodation of sixty, were erected; the old school-court was given over to women's station classes, and we saw scope for the realisation of our wildest dreams. The work amongst the men was increasing in a similar proportion. Mr. Wang, who was in charge when we arrived at Hwochow, was now appointed Deacon of the Church, and afterwards Elder. We soon recognised in him a man of no ordinary influence. Like Barnabas, he was "a good man filled with the Holy Spirit," and like him might well be called the "Son of Consolation."

The large numbers who were baptized upon profession of faith each year entailed many responsibilities—new families to be visited, more visitors to be received, marriages and funerals to be attended. Cases of persecution, real or supposed, called for many hours of patient listening, and, withal, the constant stream of city women who desired to inspect all that was going on, parents to see children in the school, friends and relatives of opium patients, who lost no chance of visiting the member of the family under treatment, changed the once quiet house into a beehive of activity.

In many Shansi houses there is a large, well-built room, open to north and south, which is set apart for the observance of the prescribed family rites connected with ancestral worship. Here are the wooden ancestral tablets, image of the soul and tangible symbol, erected to the memory of the deceased, affording thereby a fixed object for filial piety. This room on our compound was dedicated as a church for public worship; enlarged once, and again the second time, it still proved too small for our growing congregation.

The strain attendant on such a rapid development was severe, but each year found us supplied with increasingly able help from our Chinese co-workers. We found ourselves driven to the practical testing of the principle: "When the pressure of the work is too heavy, then extend the work," and we found it to be sound and workable. Each term some extra responsibility was thrown off on to the shoulders of willing helpers, that we ourselves might be free to undertake fresh enterprises.

MRS. HSI'S SECOND GIFT

"It is Jesus who has introduced into virtue a passion before which vice is not condemned but consumed as by fire."—Rev. Carnegie Simpson.

> Round the cape of a sudden came the sea,
> And the sun looked over the mountain's rim:
> And straight was a path of gold for him,
> And the need of a world of men for me."
>   Robert Browning.

CHAPTER IX

MRS. HSI'S SECOND GIFT

BEING AN ACCOUNT OF HER LIFE FROM WIDOWHOOD

ONE DIRECT result of the lack of foreign workers was the appointment of Mrs. Hsi to the oversight of the women's work in Chaocheng. During her husband's lifetime she had been eager to learn all she could, and had with difficulty mastered some of the Chinese characters. She often expressed to him her desire to learn more, but he told her to remember that the need for her to attend to the domestic side of the large establishment at the Middle Eden was essential, and her life until his death was largely a busy domestic one.

Not entirely, however, was this the case. When it became necessary to open a Refuge for Women in the city of Hungtung, it was to his wife that the Pastor looked for help, and she, there and in other places, did a truly Christlike work. It was in the city of Hsugo that she accomplished her most difficult task. It seemed as if the devil had a special power there, and Pastor Hsi was almost in despair. Man after man, amongst them some of his most trusted helpers, fell into sin, or were overcome by difficulties in that place.

How to hold it at all was a problem. He solved it by sending his wife, and alone she went to live six days' journey from the place where he was, and for the first time the work in Hsugo was successful.

Almost immediately after her return home, Pastor Hsi developed the illness from which he never recovered. He was at work on some Refuge accounts when he felt unwell, and his spirit became conscious that the messenger had come with a command "that he must prepare for a change of life, for his Master was not willing that he should be so far from Him any longer."

For nearly six months he lingered still, making preparations for the journey ahead; he gave directions for the temporary closing of the Refuges, recognising, doubtless, that the time while he was still on earth, but unable to exercise control, might be an even more perilous period than that which would follow his death. Mrs. Hsi herself fell ill, and so seriously that her life was at one time despaired of. She was barely able to stand the fatigue of the public funeral to which hundreds gathered, yielding to their grief and sobbing as children who had lost a parent. She herself was bowed with sorrow, for they had been truly one in God's service, but strength was sent to her through a dream in which she saw her husband, in glory beyond her imagining, and with him the boy who had been their only son and had died in childhood. When she desired to join them he rebuked her, saying: "Nay, but you must return"; and obedient, she turned her back on the heavenly glory and faced "the need of a world" of sin.

SCRIPTURE TESTIMONY
Pray for those who mistreat you
MATTHEW 5:44 · LUKE 6:28

Mrs. Hsi was now to realise to the full the unfortunate position of a childless widow. According to the custom of the country, the nearest male relative on her husband's side should have been her protector, but this duty devolved on a nephew who was an opium smoker, gambler, and unregenerate heathen, and what should have been protection took the form of persecution.

Elder Si, her brother-in-law, took over the control of the opium refuges and the preparation of the medicine used. Days of prayer and fasting always preceded the compounding of the drugs which were prepared in Pastor Hsi's own home, and sent out in the form of pills. It was in connection with the medicine that Mrs. Hsi's first difficulties occurred. Large quantities of the various ingredients were stored at Middle Eden, and the said nephew claimed possession of this stock, declaring his intention of defending his rights by stabbing any one who dared to touch it.

The time came when the drugs were required, and arrangements were quietly made for the removal of the material to the home of Elder Si. Before touching the goods, Mrs. Hsi called the young man to her, and addressing him by name told him to fetch his knife, as she intended to carry out her husband's wishes and supply the Refuges with the necessary medicine without delay. Abashed, and half-ashamed by her self-confidence and dignity, he muttered excuses and left her presence with an apology.

Nevertheless, it required fill her wits and most of her time to prevent this ne'er-do-weel from robbing her of all she possessed. Opium he would eat, his gambling habits were strong, and how could she prevent him from stealing that which, as one of the family, he could partially claim as his own? The problem weighed upon her mind and she decided that division of the land, each taking half the produce of the farm, was the only solution. Even so she was not safe; there is a Chinese proverb which says: "It is hard to deal with a thief who is one of the family," and she proved it to be true. If she left home for a few days she would return to find her door broken open, her clothes stolen, and her grain visibly less. Although the Chinese law would offer her redress, she, by reason of Christian principle and the example of her husband, never appealed for help to an earthly tribunal, but daily prayed: "Lord, have mercy on him, and change his heart."

In the early days of her faith, Mrs. Hsi had earnestly desired to unbind her feet as witness that she was a Christian, but her husband, fearful lest any should be misled to regard Christianity as conformity to foreign customs rather than to a change of heart, was strongly opposed to her doing so. He strictly forbade the binding of children's feet, but saw no need for outward change of shoe in the foot already disfigured. During his lifetime she yielded to his wish, but after his death refused to let her mature judgment be held in abeyance by the dead hand of the past, and did that which she felt was a testimony to many of her weaker sisters. She unbound her feet and adopted a normal shoe and sock, and many who had made her supposed attitude on the question an excuse, now followed her example. In order to give the Gospel to Hwochow Mrs. Hsi had parted with the most valuable of her worldly goods, and when the call came for the second great renunciation in response to the need for a woman worker in Chaocheng, she was ready to move into that city, knowing as she did so, that by leaving the family home she would finally close the way of return. She well knew that no seal on the door would prevent her nephew from stealing her goods, and her worst fears were realised when, a few years later, on the occasion of the erection of a memorial stone to Pastor Hsi, she revisited what had once been Middle Eden. All was gone, and she was thankful to hurry away and leave the scene that could only cause her pain.

On entering her new sphere of work, the missionaries at Hwochow assured her that all the love and sympathy which she had promised Mr. Taylor years before should be given to the first ladies who came to that city, was now to be bestowed on her. The loyal affection of the Chinese Church was hers, for she is regarded by them with an admiration and reverence which they consider the right of so worthy a woman. She knew that she could count upon a welcome, but it was a costly step.

City and village visiting, weekly classes for inquirers, and a Women's Opium Refuge occupy Mrs. Hsi's time in Chaocheng. A sentence easy to write, but only He to Whom the offering is made can know the cost at which ladies, with the refinements of their class, give themselves to the Christlike work of rescuing the opium sots who find their way to the Refuge. Women of the lowest moral type at times appear, dirty, coarse, and repulsive, and yet gladly and graciously they are received. The lady in charge will sleep with them in order to comfort and pray with them during the night watches, and no service is too menial for these saintly women to render. The impression made is never forgotten by those to whom they minister; and even if they return again to the ways of sin, the vision of that gentle lady with her kind heart will remain, a reflection, faint it may be, yet a reflection of the love of God, ever ready to welcome the wanderer from the far country.

THE STORY OF AN OPIUM SMOKER

"I know that, because of this money-grasping, trade-compelling feature of England's dealings with my country, millions of wretched people of China have been made more miserable; stalwart men and women have been made paupers, vagrants, and the lowest of criminals; and hundreds of thousands of the weaker ones of my race— mainly among the women—have been sent to suicide graves. All this because gold and territory are greater in the eyes of the British Government, than the rights and bodies of a weak people."—H. E. Li Hung-chang.

> "O my brothers and all my friends,
> If you would hearken to good advice,
> Avoid the poppy juice for ever and aye,
> As it is a plague most noxious and vile!
> It will eat out your minds,
> It will rot away your vitals,
> It will shrivel up your bowels,
> It will make you walk as a leper,
> It will cast you into prison,
> It will send you to your death!"
> H. E. Li Hung-chang.

CHAPTER X

THE STORY OF AN OPIUM SMOKER

THE FIRST man to enter the Opium Refuge in Hwochow, as patient, was named Fan of the village of Southern Springs. He came from a once wealthy clan, now reduced through opium smoking to comparative poverty. He had not yet reached the stage of positive want, but that condition is never far from the habitual heavy smoker, and should he continue a few years longer, beggary will be the ultimate fate of his wife and family.

The temptation was at his very door, for all the best-watered land surrounding Southern Springs was given up to poppy cultivation. During the time when the plant was in flower, the village nestled amidst some hundreds of acres of exquisite iridescent bloom. The beauty was short-lived, even as the seeming prosperity of the grower, and but a few days later Southern Springs stood amidst bare brown fields of dry poppy heads, scarred by the cutter's knife, exuding in thick drops the poisonous juices—a striking picture in the eyes of all men of the fate awaiting the smoker, who, lulled by the insidious charm of the fascinating drug, would finally be the only one unable to see himself a hopeless, helpless, degraded wreck.

At the close of three weeks' treatment in the Refuge, Fan returned home a new creature, restored in body and mind, and with a heart renewed in hope. In his own immediate family were several members, victims as

himself of the deadly drug, and amongst these was his nephew, adopted
into the family on the footing of a son since death had robbed him of
the last boy who might pay the filial sacrifice of tears and lamentations
at his tomb. Moreover, his wife's keen intelligence and strong will were
gradually being subjugated by a growing apathy, result of her secret habit.
On these two Fan urged a plea to give the Refuge a trial, and his nephew,
impressed by the evident good result in his uncle's case and the assurance
that the treatment had induced very slight suffering, pronounced himself
willing to try the experiment; his wife, on the other hand, repudiated
with scorn any such suggestion. Another few weeks saw the young man
return to Southern Springs loud in praise of all he had seen and heard in
Hwochow. He recounted all his experiences, every detail of the treatment,
the number of pills swallowed, and the care with which the strength of
the pills was graded from the powerful "Pill of life" to the lesser "Pill of
strength" and the final "Pill of restoration."

He also knew by heart a number of verses from the New Testament, and
could sing hymns written by Pastor Hsi on the subjects of salvation and the
sin of opium smoking, several of which numbered twelve verses in length.

All this caused much stir in the village, and became the general subject of
conversation when the men were home from the fields, during the twilight
hour devoted to social intercourse. He was referred to as a competent
authority on all matters relating to the ways and habits of those "foreign
devils" who went to and fro between the various stations which they had
opened, and even penetrated into the villages amongst the homes of any
who were rash enough to risk having them under their roof.

Both uncle and nephew had secretly entirely changed their opinion
concerning the foreigner and the Christian doctrine which he inculcated.
Fear had given place to confidence, and one or other would frequently
walk the four miles to Hwochow on a week day, or better still on Sunday,
to sit an hour with the Refuge-keeper, whom it was hard indeed not to
trust, and who always had some good matter to unfold and kind, earnest
words with which to help a man in the hour when his old vice threatened
to ensnare his soul afresh. Little sympathy was to be gained at home. Mrs.
Fan still took opium, endangering her husband's and nephew's principles

as they returned, weary from work, to a room reeking with the odour so attractive to them.

She was a woman of no ordinary character, exceptionally intelligent, strong-minded and wilful, capable in every duty which falls to the woman's share in the home; by nature hard working and ambitious, in physique of a pronounced Jewish type. Not easily led, and impossible to drive, she flew into such a passion when her husband ventured to tell her that two lady missionaries had arrived, and were prepared to receive women as patients in the Hwochow Refuge, and gave such rein to her tongue that he, poor man, was thankful to escape beyond earshot of her loud recriminations and curses.

If his words were silenced we may believe that his actions were speaking louder and more effectually, for influences stronger than the woman realised were even now at work, preparing to overturn all her preconceived prejudices and hatred of Christianity and its followers.

The climax came more suddenly than could have been anticipated, revealing to herself and others the extraordinary change of viewpoint which had been silently working during weeks of apparently unchanged opposition.

On returning from the fields one evening, Fan found his wife in an unusual state of activity, whilst the three little girls who constituted his family formed a tearful group on the *kang*. With characteristic abruptness Mrs. Fan delivered the information: "I am preparing to go to the city Opium Refuge." Scarcely able to credit her statement the husband stood aghast, and she explained: "It is no good, the children are taking it too."

A terrible statement, yet true, for whereas she knew that she had often pacified the tiny baby's fretfulness by puffing a few whiffs of the smoke into its mouth, she had that day made the discovery that, as soon as she herself lay down to sleep off the effect of her dose, the two elder girls would seize on the opium pipe and share all they could get from it, so that already, unknown to herself, the craving was well developed in them.

To the Refuge they must all go, and the next evening saw a cart at the door into which were being stowed various bundles of clothing wrapped in blue-and-yellow cloths, each bundle having attached to it a small piece of scarlet cotton to ensure luck on the journey. Flour and millet for food, and other necessaries were piled up behind the cart, and the children were packed inside and told to keep quiet, for they were leaving at night to avoid the jeers of the villagers. The father sat upon the shafts, the mother cross-legged inside, and after an hour's drive the city gates were sighted, and soon the party was welcomed at the Mission House.

A very few days in the Refuge served to largely alter the tenor of Mrs. Fan's mind. The woman who took charge of her was a kind, confidence inspiring body, with nothing of the "foreign devil" about her. She would hear no harm of the missionaries, and flatly denied that children were enticed on to the premises to be done to death by foul means, or that the foreigner's blue eye could see corpses in their coffins, or that magic incantations were used by means of which all who drank their tea must become their followers.

All these questions and many others relating to the personal character of the strange beings were asked during the long night watches when sleep evades the opium patient, and the nurse helps to while away the dreary hours by satisfying her curiosity. Then at dawn the longed-for dose of medicine is administered, after a prayer that the "medicine may heal her body, and the blood of Jesus cleanse her soul," and she may settle to a doze which daily becomes more natural and peaceful as the body returns to a normal condition of being.

Mrs. Fan saw that much was introduced by the foreigner in the wake of Christianity which her alert mind recognised as being all to the advantage of women. Even the old Refuge-keeper could read a little, but she was quite dull and slow, whereas without much trouble Mrs. Fan herself could master quite a number of new characters every day, and a few hours had been enough for the initial lesson of reading the large print rhyme:

"There is but one true God, the Heavenly Father He,
Who feeds and clothes and pities me.
The only Saviour, too, who can my sins forgive,
I trust and hearken to His word,
Jesus my Lord and Saviour.
Jesus loves the sinner, Jesus pities me,

He gave His life, He washed me clean,
He verily hath loved me."

It was quite evident that a certain amount of education lay within her own grasp, and quite unlimited possibilities were open to her three daughters. The sinfulness of binding up the feet of girls was touched upon, and a strong determination took form in her mind that her girls should be among the first who would have natural feet in the neighbourhood, in spite of the lurking fear that all three might be left as old maids upon her hands if no man might be found bold enough to risk the disgrace of a wife with normal feet. A short length of white cotton material was procured, and the three little ones were soon free of compressing bandages, each wearing a pair of calico socks and little red-and-yellow shoes, ornamented on the toe with a grinning, whiskered, tiger's face.

These girls were all destined to lives of signal usefulness in the Church. Two of them labour still as teachers and evangelists among their own people; the third was early prepared by intense suffering and deep wrongs to be removed by death to the realm where the "wicked cease from troubling and the weary are at rest."

THE GREAT FURNACE FOR A GREAT SOUL

"Happy the pure in heart, for they shall see God."

"A white bird, she told him once, looking at him gravely. A bird which he must carry in his bosom across a crowded public place—his own soul was like that!

"Would it reach the hands of his good genius on the opposite side, unruffled and unsoiled?"—Walter Pater.

"To radiate the heat of the affections into a clod, which absorbs all that is poured into it, but never warms beneath the sunshine of smiles or the pressure of hand or lip—this is the great martyrdom of sensitive beings—most of all in that perpetual *auto-da-fe* where young womanhood is the sacrifice."—O. W. Holmes.

CHAPTER XI

THE GREAT FURNACE FOR A GREAT SOUL

BEING THE STORY OF AI DO

MRS. FAN's second daughter came into the world under the shadow of sorrow, for apart from the fact that she was a girl, whereas a boy had been ardently desired, her first lusty yells revealed the fact that she was born with a tooth visible. This was well known by every woman in the village to indicate antagonism to her mother's life, and disaster would surely ensue were she not promptly drowned or thrown out to perish by the riverside.

Her fate seemed sealed, but that a woman seeing what a dear little baby she was, was moved with pity, and declared herself willing to take the responsibility of asserting that the child was hers in order that the demons which were ordering these events might be deceived, and thus her real mother would escape the fate which threatened her life, if the baby were not killed.

An incredible amount of ingenuity is expended in China on deceptions practised to mislead the *gwei* or demon, whose influence you have cause to fear. Being a malignant spirit, his object is to hurt that which you specially value, therefore it is well to deceive him into thinking that your precious son is only a useless girl, or even a little animal. This is not difficult to manage, for the *gwei*, though powerful to work evil, is a simple creature, and it is sufficient for him to see earrings dangling from your boy's ears to make him think he sees a girl, or if you call the child by some such name as "puppy," "little pig," "kitten," or "goat," he will quite fail to perceive that the object of your affection is two legs short of what one might be led to expect.

When a *gwei* has really determined to injure your child, it is sometimes necessary to kill a dog and wrap your boy in its skin, that it may be perfectly evident to the whole spirit world that if you are bestowing any affection, it is only on a valueless beast. In the case of Mrs. Fan's little girl, no *gwei* could reasonably be supposed to attach much value to her, and it was therefore sufficient for this neighbour to pronounce herself willing to stand in the place of a mother. She was allowed to live, and with painful frankness given the name of "One too many."

SCRIPTURE TESTIMONY
Holy Spirit convicts people of their sin
JOHN 16:8

After the month spent in the Opium Refuge, Mrs. Fan often saw the lady missionaries either at Hwochow or in her own house, and when they were joined by a lady who had no previous knowledge of the Chinese language, Mrs. Fan was asked if little "One too many" might come and live with the missionary so that her childish prattle should help the newcomer in recognizing the difficult sounds and tones. She was now eight years old and permission was readily granted, so to Hwochow she went and became an inmate of the Christian household there, her name being altered to the now appropriate one of "greatly loved"—in Chinese, Ai Do.

The years passed by, and little Ai Do won the love and approval of all. She received her education in the girls' school, and there grew up in her ambition to be a teacher, as her elder sister was. At fourteen years of age she sat one Sunday evening reading her Bible, and came to the words: "The Lord seeth not as man seeth; man looketh on the outward appearance, the Lord looketh on the heart." She stopped and pondered, realising with the force that can only come with conviction of the Spirit of God, that while in "the outward" no one had fault to find with her, yet the Lord looking on the heart saw her full of sin and unreconciled to Him. In that hour her peace was made, and henceforth she served and trusted God through all the vicissitudes of her short life. She remained a pupil in the school until the year 1900, when Miss Stevens and Miss Clarke went to Taiyüanfu, never to return. It was a reign of terror during which rapine and murder stalked unhindered through the land, and young women fled to the remotest districts where they might claim a shelter.

The matter of Ai Do's marriage had been under consideration for some time, she having now reached the age when custom exacts that this important matter should be settled. Various suitors presented themselves, but in most cases there was some hitch which prevented the engagement from being finally settled. In one case the man lived on the other side of the river, and this would cause difficulty in the girl's frequent journeys from one home to the other; in another, the matter of the sum required as dowry could not be finally fixed; in a third, she would have been required to worship idols.

Amongst the number was a young man, favoured by Mrs. Fan but known as a wild and dissolute youth, and the missionaries who had cared for Ai Do so many years refused their consent to the engagement. Now they were dead, and Mrs. Fan had scope for the exercise of the domineering will which made her ruler of the home, for while she was an enthusiastic follower of the Church she had never given evidence of personal conversion.

It was certainly advisable that a young woman of Ai Do's age should not be unmarried at that difficult time. Christians went in daily peril of their lives, and the soldier was scarcely less to be dreaded than the Boxer.

"No one uses good iron to make nails, and no one will use a good man to make a soldier," says a Chinese proverb, which has been proved to be only too true in many cases.

Hastily, and almost secretly, the formalities of the engagement were performed, cards were exchanged which fixed the contract, and the earrings, rings, and silk and satin garments were brought from the bridegroom's home. Ai Do had heard much of this man, and his reputation was such as to cause her the gravest misgivings.

The household which she was to enter as a bride would not require her to join in the offering of nuptial sacrifices to idols because her future mother-in-law had come under the sound of the Gospel, but more than this can scarcely be said. The son to whom she was engaged had been brought up on a regime of such extreme indulgence as can only be met with amongst an Oriental people. His mother had never once restrained him in a childish selfishness nor a manly vice. From a spoilt, inconsiderate, wilful childhood he passed to a cruel, passionate, licentious manhood; finally, he took to opium smoking and ruin threatened the home. His mother reaped a bitter harvest of sorrow from the planting of those wasted years, and now her urgent plea was: "My son is good at heart, and a virtuous bride will soon work a reform in him."

Every relation and friend and neighbour had a say in the transaction, only Ai Do must not be consulted, and though she weep and plead to be left unmarried for a time yet, her tears and supplications can cause no effect. In vain were the silver ornaments and fine clothes displayed before her; she refused to take food and wept bitterly, not with the conventional tears of the Chinese girl bewailing her virginity and begging that she may not be torn from the shelter of her maiden home, but with a real horror of the fate which awaited her.

The day dawned when she was dressed in the scarlet bridal clothes, a voluminous embroidered satin gown over all; this came with the sedan chair which was to carry her to her future home, being hired for the occasion. Scarlet shoes were on her feet, a high tinsel crown on her head, and covering her tear-stained face was a scarlet veil. In accordance with the custom which demanded that the forehead of the bride must be perfectly smooth, her front hair had been dragged out by the roots and left her with an aching head.

At last all was ready, and she was in the embroidered sedan chair and caught the last glimpse of the familiar faces. They disappear, and alone she meets a cruel, loveless, unknown world.

A Chinese village wedding is a terrible ordeal for the bride. Her life until that day has been guarded from every contact with the outer world, and she has never spoken with a man outside the family circle. Her arrival at her mother-in-law's home is the signal for a wild rush of rough men to surround her chair. The curtain is lifted, insolent faces stare, her personal appearance is commented upon in vile terms, her feet being specially noticed because the artificial compression of this member has resulted in giving it sexual importance in a woman's appearance. Ai Do had a normal, unbound foot, and had to listen to lewd insinuations levelled at her on this subject. All the while she must patiently sit and wait until the appointed women of the bridegroom's family are ready to conduct her indoors. The waiting is often for a considerable time, for these new relations are going to make her feel that she is a most unimportant and undesirable person, and her mother-in-law is not even going to see her until the next day; moreover, the longer she waits, the greater her chances of longevity.

When at last she is told to leave her chair she is followed by a crowd, and holding the end of a scarlet sash which is thrust into her hand, she finds herself in a courtyard where the ceremony is to take place.

In accordance with the contract made by the middleman, she is not asked to worship heaven and earth nor the tablets of her husband's ancestors, but two cups of wine are placed on the table, and she and her bridegroom must each take one and sip the wine, the cups being joined together by a scarlet thread. When this ceremony is over, she follows her bridegroom to a room, still led by the sash, and when he enters he stands upon the *kang* and by walking around it demonstrates his position as head of the new home.

Meanwhile the chair-bearers are clamouring for her dress, as another young woman is waiting for the same gown and chair, and delay may cause trouble. The bride is assisted on to the *kang* by the women, her husband having departed to make merry with his friends, and the ragged opium smokers who carried her there leave, one wearing the crown of tinsel on his head, laughing and joking at much which they have seen and heard. From the moment that she is seated upon the *kang*, the bride becomes the centre of attraction to an insulting crowd. Her shoes are stolen, but knowing that this is likely she has provided herself with additional pairs. For hours she sits there and hears the remarks made.

One will whisper that she is married to an irresponsible idiot, others will tell her that he is blind or dumb, and knowing how often the middlemen deceive, she waits with dread the moment when she will see for herself more than she was able to do on arrival. At last the room is cleared, and she has to face the final ordeal when she is left alone with a totally unknown man. Even the hours of darkness are not respected, and every youngster in the village has the right to enter the courtyard at any hour of the night, tear down the paper windows, and heap shame upon her head.

Christianity and the influence of the foreigner has done much to revolutionise the wedding customs, but all this and more was endured by Ai Do, and she found herself withal the wife of a depraved and vicious man.

It was indeed a deliverance when the Hwochow girls' school reopened and Ai Do was invited to teach in place of her elder sister, whose family claims had increased so as to prevent her holding the post as formerly. School was opened in a small courtyard which adjoined our own, and twenty girls entered as pupils. Ai Do had all the characteristics of a natural leader, and she easily controlled the girls and was much beloved by them, for she had a kind disposition and the hidden sorrows of her life had made her both strong and tender.

I think that her life in school was a time of unmixed happiness to her, but the holidays had to be faced and contact with the man whom she could only strive not to hate. His opium smoking habits increased, and the pinch of poverty was felt in the home from which he was able to steal so cunningly every article of value which might be exchanged for money and spent on the drug.

A great joy came into Ai Do's life with the birth of a little son, and she realised for the first time that matrimony was not solely a horror, since it brought so much compensation in its train. The child was publicly dedicated to God, and was its mother's joy for six brief months.

At the end of that time, in the hot weather, it sickened with dysentery, and in spite of her prayers and entreaties that she might be allowed to deal with the disease as she had seen me deal with similar ailments, she had to endure the torture of seeing it operated upon by a heathen Chinese doctor, whose method of treatment was to use long needles which he ran into its tender flesh. The needles were of course unclean, and the child's death was doubtless hastened by the shock thus sustained.

She was spared the last sorrow of seeing its body thrown out to be devoured by dogs and wolves through the fortunate advent of her father, who insisted at her request that decent burial be given. This was a cause of thankfulness for her to her life's end.

A year later, when her second son was born, the home was in a pitiful condition. All the land which provided daily bread for the family was gambled away, furniture and clothes had been sold or pawned for opium, the wages she earned were all turned to the same use, and the poorest, coarsest food was all that was procurable at a time when her strength was quite insufficient to the strain imposed upon it.

As soon as the required month of purification was over, she returned to us and then received all the care that love could suggest, but we soon saw that she was going to escape from our poor, inadequate efforts to protect and comfort her, into the care of the only One who could save her from further sorrow. Phthisis took a rapid hold of her constitution, and her strength daily declined. During this time she for the first time opened her heart, and spoke out her sorrows and sufferings and those deepest wrongs she had suffered which women have from time immemorial hidden as a shameful secret. She spoke it all out now, and left me with a determination that henceforth any one placed as she was should find an advocate and protector in me to the extent of my ability.

Three months later she was carried back to her home, a dying woman, to end her days. We were able to ride out and see her almost daily, and once we found her very happy because in a dream she had seen a messenger who called to her to cross the river, and when she shrank back I had been there to assure her that angels would receive her to her Heavenly Home.

That day her husband came into the room, and in my presence she for the last time pleaded with him to leave the ways of sin and seek forgiveness through repentance. To our care she committed her child, asking that we would see that it was brought up as a Christian, and she also begged us to insist on a Christian burial for herself. To the schoolgirls she sent the message that they must meet her in her Master's presence, and a few hours later "the bells of the city rang out for joy, and it was said to her: 'Enter into the joy of thy Lord.'" The wail that went up from the schoolgirls when I told them, I shall not forget; she was the first of our company to pass over. Two days later the pupils of her class and ourselves gathered with the family for a simple service in the courtyard of her home. On the coffin the words were written at her own request, "Until He come"—symbolic of the hope which sustained her through those years of suffering, and kept her eyes ever upward turned to the promise of the great day of deliverance. A congregation of some hundreds assembled to see the unique sight of so many girls mourning for a teacher and following the bier to the border of the village. The girls and their parents showed their appreciation of Ai Do and her work by presenting a large banner to the school in her memory. It was unveiled on their behalf by the elders of the Church, and above the names of one hundred girls who had been her pupils were inscribed the words: "She rests from her labours, and her works do follow her."

We returned to take up the work which she had left, but with heavy hearts, and the school and my study seemed empty without her presence. I missed her help in consultation over difficulties and dealings with the raw material which came into our hands at the beginning of each term.

Who could replace her? Her friend and companion who had helped her during the past months was the only one to whom I could look, and she was seemingly of too retiring a disposition to bear such responsibility; but the "trees of the Lord are full of sap," and if a leaf has fallen there is always a fresh one developing to replace it, and Ling Ai was preparing for a development which was going to make her that which she still is, my faithful and beloved fellow-missionary in this place. With her quiet, gentle spirit she has won the confidence of her pupils, and made possible for me that which apart from her comradeship would have been impossible, the establishment of a large school and training-college where in happy fellowship Chinese young women are working together for the women and girls of their country.

THE POWERS OF DARKNESS

"What name hast thou? And he said, Legion!"

"Whensoever the impure spirit goeth out from the man it passeth through waterless places seeking rest; and not finding it there, it saith—

"I will return unto my house whence I came out:

"And coming, findeth it empty, swept and adorned. Then goeth it and taketh along with itself other spirits more wicked than itself—seven, and entering it, findeth its dwelling there; and the last state of that man becometh worse than the first."—The Gospel according to Luke.

CHAPTER XII

THE POWERS OF DARKNESS

BEING A RECORD OF SOME OBSERVATIONS
IN DEMONOLOGY

T HE CHINAMAN, though perhaps the most materialistic of Eastern-
ers, is no exception to his neighbours in the large place which the
occult takes in his outlook. For him, the physical world is peopled
with spirits good and evil, capable of exercising the most far-reaching
influences on the fortunes of men. These spiritual beings are bound up
in the forces of nature, and combine to constitute that geomantic system
known by the Chinese as *Feng-shui* (wind and water), by reference to
which, matters of human life, inasmuch as they are designed to court the
good influences and avoid those which are inauspicious to the man, the
time, and the place, are decided.

The Chinaman can never experience the feeling of complete solitude
which the Westerner knows in wild and lonely places; for him the hillside, the ravine, and the mountain gorge are peopled with presences best
described as fairies, though in nothing resembling the light-hearted beings
which this description generally conveys to the Western mind. To him they
present the appearance of aged, venerable beings, short of stature, with
white beards. Country, town, and human habitations are alike haunted

by psychic beings whose condition cannot be exactly expressed by the word *spirit*, neither form of Chinese belief admitting of the conception of a pure spirit without matter.

These beings may be grouped into three classes. *Gwei* is the term most constantly used by the common people to indicate the being whose influence is feared by all, and who receives from every family some measure of propitiatory sacrifice. We read in the *li chao chuan*,[1] or Divine Panorama, that "every living being, no matter whether it be a man or an animal, a bird or a quadruped, a gnat or a midge, a worm or an insect, having legs or not, few or many, all are called *gwei* after death."

Apart from these are the *shen*, which have been defined as *émanations de la nature personifiées*, not, as the *gwei*, spirits of the dead, but an emanation of nature clothed with a personality. They possess varying degrees of intelligence and power. Their interest is not only in the affairs of men, to the knowledge of which they have access, but also in the secret springs of human action. They reside in man as well as amongst men, and witness to his good or evil works before the tribunal of heaven. The classics of Chinese literature, recognising this, urge upon readers the duty of decorum, purity, and care even when unseen by human eyes and according to the teachings of Confucius; one of the characteristics of the Princely Man is the discipline he will exercise upon himself when alone.

Other spiritual beings are those who, by their ascetic practices, have attained to a life higher than that of humanity; it will endure through many centuries, and they are free to live in the pleasant places of the earth with considerable licence to enjoy good things, yet free from the material claims which govern human life. These are known by the term *hsien*, and are referred to above as fairies. Each and all of these beings touch the destinies of man at various points.

It is, however, in the important events of life— birth, marriage, and

---

1   The *Precious Regulations*, a book written under the Sung Dynasty. Its main tenets are derived from Buddhism, though some writers inscribe the book among the Taoist documents. Its sub-title explains its contents: "A precious record of examples published by the mercy of Yu Di (the Jade Emperor to whom is entrusted the superintendence of the world, the Jupiter of the Taoists), that men and women may repent them of their faults and make atonement for their sins." It includes a description of the Ten Courts of Hell and the judgments pronounced therein.

death—that the interference of the spirits is strongest, and such occasions are used by the sorcerer as a means of extorting money from his unfortunate victim. In the *Divine Panorama*, we read that: "It is not uncommon at the time of reincarnation to see women asking to be allowed to avenge themselves in the form of *gwei* before being changed into men. On their case being examined, it is found that as young women they have been seduced or have been betrayed in other ways, such as the husband refusing after marriage to fulfil his promise to support the girl's parents, and in consequence of her disgrace the woman has committed suicide." From that moment terror has dogged the steps of her husband, and he has gone in hourly fear of sickness, accident, or sudden death. If he be a student, the day of examination presents terrors calculated to ensure failure, for he knows that the *gwei* has power to hold his mind in subjection so that he cannot write his competitive essay. The only hope, he has of release is the taking of a vow, whereby he undertakes to study and make known *The Divine Panorama* or *precious record* transmitted to men to move them, being a record of examples published by the mercy of Yu Di, that men and women living in this world may repent them of their faults, and make atonement for their sins. The punishments described include all the most painful tortures of which Chinese ingenuity can conceive. Truly, idols are the work of man's hands, and they that make them are like unto them!

Sculptural art also has left nothing undone to represent the god as animated by the worst passions of man, but skill and ingenuity must inevitably stop short of the final act necessary to convince man that communication is possible between him and the spirit world. In order to bridge this chasm a class of men and women called sorcerers (*mo-han and sheng-po*) has come into being, whose work it is to be the spokesmen of the gods. With deliberate intent and elaborate ritual they develop the mediumistic gift, and learn how to attain conditions of frenzy and of trance during which period the body is controlled by a spiritualistic force. Not only as the medium of the gods, but also as a resting-place for longer or shorter periods to the homeless, unclean spirit, do these sorcerers serve. At tremendous physical cost—for the medium is never long-lived—they accumulate great wealth, exorbitant sums being demanded in recognition of services rendered when freeing a family or village from the visitations of a tormenting *gwei*. When sickness enters his home, the Chinaman's instinct is to attribute it to any cause rather than a natural one; his appeal on such occasions is to the sorcerer whose time is largely occupied in giving what is called medical advice, but is in reality the practising of the rites of exorcism. Sometimes he will declare that the spirit of a sick person has strayed from the body, and means will be set on foot to secure its return. A woman I know, whose boy had apparently died from typhoid fever, was told that his spirit had been enticed away by a god whose shrine was built on the mountain side near the city where she lived. She took the child's coat and walked to the temple; here, standing before the idol, she burned incense and begged that the boy's spirit might be restored to her. Holding the child's coat open to receive it, she swayed to and fro, and with heart-rending cries besought it to return. She waited until she felt her request had been granted, and with a movement as though to enfold the little wandering ghost, she clasped the coat in her arms and swiftly returning home, laid it upon the lifeless body. The child revived, and is alive to this day.

Frequently, after supplication to the gods, the clothes of the patient are carefully weighed; a procession is then formed in which one of the sorcerers holds a mirror directed backwards, others, wearing scarlet aprons, carry brooms and with slow and mystic movements sweep widely on either side with the intent of gathering up the wandering soul. Meanwhile crackers are fired to the weird sound of a minor, falsetto lilting. After a considerable journey over the countryside they return to prove the success of their venture. For this the clothes of the sick man must be reweighed to see whether the weight of the spirit has been added to that of the patient's garments. Should the smallest discrepancy be detected all is well, and after feasting and opium the *mo-han* pockets his fee and departs, frequently leaving a prescription behind him, the results of which may be more or less harmful. Whatever the result, nothing will shake the faith of the people in these degraded villains, for they can, by threatening to call in the intervention of the gods on their behalf strike terror to the heart of any man, and once having sought aid of the sorcerer, the family is pitiable indeed.

In a case which came under my personal observation, the spirit of a young woman from a village at some distance from the one in which I was staying, who had recently died in childbirth, was said to have returned, having found herself in difficulties in the spirit world for lack of means to defray the necessary expenses. Illness became so prevalent that necromancers were called in and agreed that a medium must be employed. The spirit made its requirements known, and by promising the sacrifices ordained, the family passed under a bondage from which none dared to emancipate himself by omitting the prescribed rites. Night after night, at the medium's command a table was spread at the cross-roads, on which were laid the fantastic foods suitable to the requirements of the departed spirit. Gold and silver paper money was plentifully burned, crackers were fired, and following the medium, a party of men left to place earthen bowls containing grains at various corners of the roads.

Nothing but the deliverance of Christianity, or a daring known to few, can set free those who have been entangled in such practices.

I saw this medium whilst under spirit control. Before a table elaborately decorated on which incense burned, she threw herself into extraordinary contortions, quivering and shaking, her finger and thumb forming a circle, whilst the little finger vibrated continuously. She sustained a perpetual chant in the peculiar spirit voice, the minor strains of which I find it impossible to describe. A relative of the deceased acted as questioner, and she dictated the terms by the fulfilment of which the spirit consented to a reconciliation.

Another manifestation of mediumship may be found in the more or less conscious yielding of the personality to a controlling spiritualistic influence, known as *demon possession*. Remarkable cases have come under my own personal observation, and all incidents which I quote have been witnessed by foreign missionaries who are prepared to vouch for their accuracy. Those brought to my notice by reliable Chinese are too numerous to include in this book, but the fact that men and women who lay themselves open to demoniacal influences become possessed, is beyond dispute. In many cases the possession follows upon a fit of uncontrolled temper, such as is not uncommon amongst the Chinese; in others it is connected with the taking of a vow on the occasion of illness in the home, when service was promised to some particular god; or again, it has been undoubtedly connected with the neglect to completely remove idols from the home of a Christian.

In yet other cases, a spirit may take temporary possession of a human body in order to find a means of expression for some important communication, and after delivering its message leave the person unconscious of that which has taken place. An instance of this occurred in a family with which I am intimate. The eldest daughter was married into a home where she received ill- treatment from her mother-in-law. For several years she was systematically underfed and overworked, and when at last she gave birth to a son we all expected she would receive more consideration. The hatred of her mother-in-law was, however, in no degree abated, and when the child was a month old she brought her daughter a meal of hot bread in which the girl detected an unusual flavour which made her suspicious. She threw the remainder to the dog, and before many hours had passed both the unfortunate girl and the dog were dead.

Her father was away from home at the time, the young men of the family meanwhile carrying on the work of the farm. A few days later her brothers and first cousins, strong, vigorous young farmers, being together in the fields, her cousin, aged twenty-two, suddenly exhibited symptoms of distress. He trembled and wept violently. Those with him becoming alarmed at so unusual a sight went to his assistance, intending to take him home. He wept, however, the more violently, saying: "I am Lotus-bud; I was cruelly done to death. Why is there no redress?" Others of the family were by this time at hand, and recognising the effort made by the girl's spirit to communicate with her own people whom she had had no opportunity of seeing in the hour of her death, spoke directly to her, as though present. Telling her the facts of the case, they explained that all demands must remain in abeyance until her father's return, when the guilty party would be dealt with by her family whose feeling was in no sense one of indifference. In about an hour's time the attack passed, leaving the young man exhausted and unconscious of what had taken place.

The criminal law of China can only be put in action under such circumstances by the girl's own family undertaking a long and expensive lawsuit, the result of which may end in the punishment of the criminal, or may terminate in quite a different way. In this case the demands took the form of a requirement, the granting of which constituted a tacit acknowledgment of guilt. The demand in fact was that a funeral monument should be erected in memory of the dead girl. This constituted so uncalled-for an honour paid to one in her position, as to be a public recognition that redress was due to her, and a law case was avoided.

It may be remembered that in the first chapter of this book an incident is recorded of Mrs. Hsi herself being tormented by a demon which had gained its power over her, by reason of neglect to completely destroy all idols at the time when they were removed from the home. Such a case is not singular.

Our first woman patient in the Hwochow Opium Refuge became interested in the Gospel, and on her return home destroyed her idols, reserving however the beautifully carved idol shrines which she placed in her son's room. Her daughter-inlaw who occupied this room, a comely young woman, desired to become a Christian and gave us a warm welcome whenever we could go to the house. About six months later we were fetched by special messenger from a village where we were staying, to see this girl who was said to be demon possessed. We found crowds of men and women gathered to see and to hear. The girl was chanting the weird minor chant of the possessed, the voice, as in every case I have seen, clearly distinguishing it from madness. This can perhaps best be described as a voice distinct from the personality of the one under possession. It seems as though the demon used the organs of speech of the victim for the conveyance of its own voice. She refused to wear clothes or to take food, and by her violence terrorised the community. Immediately upon our entering the room with the Chinese woman evangelist she ceased her chanting, and slowly pointed the finger at us, remaining in this posture

> SCRIPTURE TESTIMONY
>
> *Demons cast out in Jesus' name*
>
> MATTHEW 8:16-17 · MATTHEW 8:28-32 · MATTHEW 9:32-34 · MARK 1:23-26 · MARK 9:20-27 · LUKE 10:17

for some time. As we knelt upon the *kang* to pray, she trembled and said: "The room is full of gwei; as soon as one goes another comes." We endeavoured to calm her, and to make her join us in repeating the sentence, "Lord Jesus, save me."

After considerable effort she succeeded in pronouncing these words, and when she had done so we commanded the demon to leave her, whereupon her body trembled and she sneezed some fifty or sixty times, then suddenly came to herself, asked for her clothes and some food, and seemingly perfectly well resumed her work. So persistently did she reiterate the statement that the demons were using the idol shrines for a refuge, that during the proceedings just mentioned her parents willingly handed over to the Christians present these valuable carvings, and joined with them in their - destruction. From this time onwards she was perfectly well, a normal, healthy young woman.

Upon recovery from illness a woman I knew yielded herself to the lord of hell for a certain period, during which time she was under a vow to wear black garments, to perform certain rites as required by the devil, and to chant instead of speaking. She told me once that she knew all I could tell her of the Lord of Heaven and of the death upon the cross of His Son, but that she served the lord of hell, and his servant she remained, only giving up her peculiar dress and manner when the time of her vow had expired.

The yielding of personality to the possession of a spirit no doubt seriously weakens the will power. Many cases are on record of those who once delivered, like the man in the Gospel from whom the evil spirit had been cast out, unconsciously again prepare the empty house to receive the evil guest, and whose latter state is worse than the former.

> SCRIPTURE TESTIMONY
>
> *Demons cast out in Jesus' name*
>
> MATTHEW 8:16-17 · MATTHEW 8:28-32 · MATTHEW 9:32-34 · MARK 1:23-26 · MARK 9:20-27 · LUKE 10:17

It was to a woman, terror of the district in which she lived, that a Chinese evangelist was called. After prayer in which he and some inquirers took part, the evil spirit in obedience to their command departed. A few weeks later on yielding to violent temper, she fell into a worse state than before. The missionary of the district was this time begged to go himself. As soon as he entered the room the woman threw herself upon the *kang*, rolling about in seemingly great agony. The Chinese helper, Mr. Li, rebuked the spirit, saying: "We ordered you to leave. Why have you returned?" "I could find no dwelling-place," was the answer, given with extraordinary rapidity, in the curious spirit voice. "Find me a place to rest, and I will leave at once." "We have come," said Li, "to command you to leave, not to find you a place." Upon this the woman laughed and clapped her hands, and in the struggle it seemed as if the powers of evil were in the ascendancy. As she still chuckled with amusement, Li said: "Let us sing a hymn," and immediately the voice replied: "I too can sing," and forthwith shouted some theatrical songs. Air. Li then prayed, but there was seemingly no power and the voice also mockingly prayed. The missionary then interposed, saying: "I have not come here to hold intercourse with demons," and forthwith authoritatively commanded the demon to leave her. There was a struggle, and she fell down unconscious on the *kang*.

She came to herself in a normal condition and apologised to the missionary for her state of deshabille. Faithfully and sternly he rebuked her for sin and for giving place to the devil. She recognised her fault, and was from that time a changed woman.

An evil spirit has been known to claim a young girl as its possession, forbidding her marriage under severe threats. It was in such a case that a demon, driven from a man who had become a Christian, went to a village eight miles distant and possessed a young woman. Speaking through her, it forbade her marriage and manifested itself in the same manner as it had done in the man from whom it came, compelling him to perpetually rub one side of his face and head until there was no hair left there. When questioned as to whence it came the demon replied by giving the name of this man, and to the question: "Why have you left him?" replied: "I have been turned out, for that man has become a Christian."

Two methods of exorcism are used by the sorcerers—defiance and bribery. The Christian method is that of commanding the evil spirit in the Name of the Lord Jesus Christ to release the victim.

Some have been set free from the power of a tormenting spirit who have not been subsequently kept free, through refusing to yield to the control

of the great Spirit of Liberty. Pastor Hsi, than whom none better understood the conflict in the Heavenly Places, in earlier days would cast out
demons from all the possessed who were brought to him, but in later years
as experience grew, he refused to do so unless idols were destroyed, and
he had reason to believe there was a sincere desire to obey the commands
of God. He doubtless saw, as others have done, the futility of temporary
relief during which, in that mysterious way so graphically described in
the Scriptures, the demon wanders in waterless places, joining himself to
others more evil than he.

Pastor Hsi learned to distinguish between the greater and the lesser
demons. With the latter he would deal summarily, but not so with the
former. "This kind," he would say, "goeth not out but by prayer and fasting;"
and thus he would prepare himself for an encounter with the powers of evil.

Young believers, doubtless impressed by the Pastor's command over
unclean spirits and perhaps sometimes eager for a similar power, were, as
in the instances recorded in the Acts of the Apostles, in serious danger.
Pastor Hsi urged them not lightly to undertake the casting out of demons.
He had been faced by the awful realities of the spirit world, and on one
occasion at least, by reason of a thoughtless word, had been troubled by
the very demon he had cast out and which attached itself to his person.

The experiences recorded here may be unfamiliar to many readers, and
some will doubtless think that madness, hysteria, or epilepsy may account
for them. To such I would suggest the following points for consideration:
Firstly, the striking, detailed resemblance between the cases seen now in
heathen lands and those recorded in the Scriptures; secondly, the complete
and lasting restoration resulting from prayer and from the command
in the Name of the Lord Jesus that the demon should depart; thirdly,
the appalling sense of the reality of the conflict with the evil one at the
moment of supreme test, as the missionary is called upon to prove his
personal faith, and to give the command which shall decide whether God
or demon remains conqueror on the field.

When the promise was given by Christ that His witnesses should cast out
demons, it was with the foreknowledge that such equipment was essential
to those who obeyed His command to disciple the nations. Let the signs

following be a reminder to weary warriors that the Captain of our salvation is actively leading His hosts; and to the indifferent and half-hearted who profess and call themselves Christians, let it be a matter for serious reflection that there exist churches in many heathen lands, the members of which have not lost their first love and faith, and against whom the enemy has come with his whole strength.

A feeble conflict may provoke a feeble resistance, but it behoves the aggressive warrior to prepare for the fight of his life when he invades the enemy's territory, where the conflict is not with "mere flesh and blood, but with the despotisms, the empires, the forces, that control and govern this dark world."

THE LIFE STORY OF PASTOR WANG

"Happy the meek;
For they shall inherit the earth."

The labourer whom Christ in His own garden
Chose to be His helpmate."

Dante.

"He went out to seek wisdom, as many a one has done, looking
for the laws of God with clear eyes to see, with a pure heart to
understand, and after many troubles, after many mistakes, after
much suffering, he came at last to the truth."—H. Fielding Hall.

CHAPTER XIII

THE LIFE STORY OF PASTOR WANG

I F PASTOR Hsi may be spoken of as the Paul of the Shansi Church, Barnabas finds his counterpart in Pastor Wang of Hwochow.

Though possessing none of the peculiar gifts which made Hsi a leader amongst foreigners and Chinese, he has exercised a remarkable personal influence upon hundreds of lives, winning by consistency and sincerity those with whom he has come in contact. On our first arrival we found him already in charge, conducting the Sunday services and generally caring for the Church members.

His unfailing courtesy, consideration, and tact simplified many difficult situations, and the exercise of his natural gift for gathering people around him and drawing out

> **SCRIPTURE TESTIMONY**
>
> *Love your enemies and do good to them*
>
> LUKE 6:32-35

the best in them soon resulted in a rapidly growing work. He was almost immediately chosen as Deacon, and before long the office of Elder was given to him. All turned to Mr. Wang in difficulty, sought his advice in perplexity, and by the unanimous desire of the Church he was in 1909 ordained Pastor at Hwochow.

He has developed his gifts in the school of adversity, for trouble overtook him in his childhood when his father died only a few years before the great famine which was to sweep over the province of Shansi. Poor they always were, and his love for his mother was intensified as he saw the self-sacrificing devotion with which she earned enough by her spinning to enable him to continue his schooling. At the age of fifteen he was married, and on the bride's arrival the falsity of the middleman through whom the engagement had been long ago contracted was revealed, for the bride was a helpless cripple and a serious burden on the already over-pressed household.

Food soon began to be scarce, for the rains failed and the prospect of the wheat harvest was poor. They endured and hoped, being mercifully saved from the knowledge that they must now enter upon a period when the inhabitants of Shansi should touch the depths of human suffering and call on death to end their woes. No pen can fully describe the horrors of that time. When summer and autumn crops had failed the rains were still withheld, and despair seized on all as they saw the impossibility of sowing the wheat for next year's harvest.

The delicate bride, unable to withstand the privations of that time, soon died, and Wang's sister was married, so that he and his mother remained alone to care for each other. The poor young sister lived but a very short while in her new home, and the circumstances of her death were so tragic that Wang felt unable to forgive the man who had been her husband. After many years, when circumstances brought this man to his home, he realised that Christ's command to forgive those who have offended against you required of him a complete change of feeling towards this once hated brother-in-law, and he invited him to share his food as a sign of forgiveness and reconciliation.

Every month the distress became more acute; weeds, leaves, bark of trees, and even some softer kinds of wood were used as food, but numbers were dying and of the one hundred and twenty families which inhabited the village, at last thirty only remained. The dead outnumbered the living, and compelled by hunger the latter were driven to sustain life by feeding on the former.

Wang saw his mother's vain endeavour to supply some kind of food on which they might subsist, and his heart was torn to see her deprive herself even now that there might be more for him.

When the famine was at its worst, the most tragic blow fell. His mother one day told him it was her wish that he should accompany several neighbours to a near village where lived a relation. In those days none dared to travel alone, lest in their weak, half-starved condition they should fall a prey to man or beast. The pretext given was the possibility of obtaining the loan of a little grain from the aunt who lived there. Beggars were many and givers few, and he wondered at his mother entertaining any hope of such good fortune.

He went, however, only to return a few hours later, empty-handed. As he entered the court yard, heart-sick with disappointment, he called for his mother and received no answer. Doors and windows were locked on the inside, and sick with apprehension he called the neighbours to his help. On bursting open the door, they saw her body swinging from a beam in the dim recesses of the cave. The errand had been an excuse to get him out of the way, while she performed this act which was the last expression of her love to him. She had chosen this solution of their impossible position, hoping that, relieved of her presence, he might be able to endure till the coming harvest.

The body, wrapped in matting, was laid in an empty cave. There was no money for a coffin, and many were waiting like hungry wolves to eat the unconfined dead; moreover, the boy and his uncle were too weak to drag the body to the burying-ground.

The months passed, and still the arid, sunbaked earth refused to bear any green thing, and the despairing people longed for rain which never came. The second year of drought had come and gone, and there was now nothing sown in the fields, but on the seventh day of the fourth moon of the fourth year of the Emperor Kwang Hsu, the longed-for rain fell and hope revived.

At this time also a stranger came to the village registering the names of survivors, and announcing that foreigners had arrived and were distributing grain that the fields might be sown for an autumn crop.

The worst of the famine was over, but the terrors of famine fever had yet to be faced, and when the longed-for grain had ripened there were in many houses none left to eat it, for whole families had been wiped out.

Wang now naturally became an inmate of his uncle's home, and gradually the conditions of greatest horror were relieved. As soon as strength had sufficiently returned, they made coffins and prepared to bury their dead, that the required rites should not be lacking which should bring consolation to those who had entered the land of shades without the necessary honours having been paid to their memory. Not only for the coffins was money required, but also to pay the fees of the geomancers who must decide the site of the graves and an auspicious day for the funeral. In this one family, thirteen coffins were made and graves dug in accordance with the following plan: The four quarterings of the celestial sphere were borne in mind, respectively governed by the Azure Dragon, Red Bird, White Tiger, and Black Tortoise, these being identified with East, West, South, and North. The graves should face the south, with White Tiger on the right and Azure Dragon on the left, as these respectively control wind and water.

On the day of the funeral the son, dressed in coarse white cloth, with unhemmed garments, white twists plaited with the hair of his queue which he wore over his chest, and his head unshaven, walked as chief mourner, the wailing relatives following the bier. In due course, paper money and other articles were burned for the use of the deceased, and fire crackers were exploded to ensure the soul and the mortal remains against the attacks of demons. The next year in early spring on the day known as *Pure Brightness*, in accordance with national custom, Wang, dressed in white, again visited and repaired the grave. For three years he wore signs of mourning in his dress, and abstained from all festivities. Thus he strove to leave undone nothing which filial piety could contrive, to make easier to his mother her sojourn in those mysterious realms whither she had passed.

For the next few years he worked as a silversmith in his uncle's shop, this latter being a generous, kindly man, on whom the responsibilities of business life sat only too lightly, for an illness revealed the fact that the profits were not sufficient to meet the interest due on the rapidly accumulating debts.

Moreover, the sick man, with failing health, had gradually acquired the use of the fatal drug known as "foreign smoke," which some years previously had been first introduced from distant lands, and was gaining ground every year as a profitable crop in the best soil. One ounce a day had become the necessary allowance for the sick man, and to Hwochow the nephew constantly went in order to buy the needful supply. He tells how he walked between the poppy fields and heard the chant which always accompanied the sowing of the plant:

> "Of ten acres, fateful plant, thou claimest eight,
> Thus only two are left for ripening grain;
> From distant lands thou wert brought here,
> And hast devoured the best of China's sons."

Of famine, of typhus, and of the raids of wild beasts, the inhabitants of Shansi had tasted the full terrors, but now this more insidious foe was working havoc in their midst. Amongst the villagers it already counted its victims: one young man had recently died as a direct result of its use, for after taking his accustomed dose he had so lain down that a portion of his wadded clothes was touching the lighted stove. Shortly after, his mother entered the cave to find this, her only son, burned to death, the charred corpse being all that remained to tell the tale. Another neighbour had gradually parted with all his possessions, and when nothing else remained on which to raise money, he took his young wife and sold her to an innkeeper in whose house she was not mistress of her actions and had no choice but to obey her purchaser. Nothing could save her, and the tragedy of that broken heart still awaits His judgment Who judgeth righteously.

The duty of preparing the pipe for his uncle devolved on the young man, and before long he himself was a victim of opium.

Meanwhile the uncle was weaker than formerly, and a neighbour strongly recommended Wang to visit the China Inland Mission station at Hwochow to ask for some medicine, and this was how he first heard the Gospel story. He was cordially received by the evangelist, and given a dose to be administered according to regulation, and told to pray earnestly for his uncle; this he conscientiously did, kneeling in the courtyard, and saying: "Heavenly Father, have mercy on my uncle." The next day, the sick man was better, and continued so for many months.

Troubles soon thickened around Mr. Wang. When his uncle died he found himself responsible for business and home, and overwhelmed by debts.

The great spiritual crisis of his life was at hand. He had from childhood pursued, by what broken light he had, an ideal which was intensely real to him. In the five relationships wherein his teachers had instructed him as to conduct, he had endeavoured to be blameless: as subject to ruler, son to father, younger brother to elder, husband to wife, and friend to friend. He had worked beyond his strength to clear himself of debt, and when his best endeavours proved futile he had sold his goods and distributed their price amongst the creditors. Having taken the vow of an ascetic, for years he was a vegetarian. Nevertheless, all had failed, and he bitterly reproached himself with having fallen into the sin of opium smoking.

> SCRIPTURE TESTIMONY
>
> *The Gospel is true and above pretense*
>
> PHILIPPIANS 1:15-18

Now it happened that a certain man, jealous of Pastor Hsi's success, opened a rival opium refuge in which he treated patients according to the Pastor's methods, but with medicine of his own making. The scheme was a contentious one, and the man himself a cause of friction and difficulty to the Christian community. It was to this Refuge that Mr. Wang, now thirty years old, poor, sad, and dispirited, came as a patient. He found here a man who, according to the established tradition of the opium refuge, received even a degraded class of men into his house in order to care for them, and performed many menial tasks in the discharge of his duty towards them. Also the good news of the Evangel was proclaimed in the house. If the preaching were not sincere but proclaimed a Christ of contention, it behoves us to rejoice that even so Christ was preached, for Mr. Wang heard something of the life of Jesus, His love, and His humility, and thought that he saw the very spirit of the doctrine exemplified in the man who ministered to these unfortunate patients. His heart was overwhelmed by the love of God; and the beauty of Christ, after which he for so many years had blindly felt, lest haply he might find, was now revealed to him. On the ninth day, for lack of money, he was obliged to cut his treatment short and return home; but henceforth nothing could separate him from the love of God.

The rumour of his conversion soon spread, and many visited the workshop where the silversmith sat at his daily occupation, questioning him, hearing his story, and taking note of the great change in him. From the first he exercised a great influence on men, and soon a few were joining with him morning and evening for prayer and reading of the Bible.

The last month of the year—a period dreaded by the Chinaman whose liabilities exceed his assets—found him in great straits. A fever had laid him low, but as soon as

SCRIPTURE TESTIMONY
God answers prayer
LUKE 18:7 · JOHN 15:7 · ACTS 12:5 · JAMES 5:15

strength returned sufficiently to sit up in bed and work he was plying his trade once more, and it was thus his creditors found him when they came to press their claims.

The Chinese universal system of debt does not allow for the exercise of mercy, as each creditor is himself a debtor, and his object in securing payments is to relieve the pressure brought to bear on himself by his own creditors. Nevertheless, the sight of the sick man forcing himself to work, and the reputation he had for integrity so affected them that they left the house again, begging him to reserve his strength and free his mind from immediate anxiety on their account. Health and strength finally returned, and intercourse was established with the Hwochow missionaries, which resulted in his baptism. By the year 1900 a group of Christian men and women formed the nucleus of a church in the village. Mr. Wang this year became a widower for the second time, the wife he had taken some years previously dying in childbirth, leaving him the care of two small children. The newborn babe it was impossible for him to rear, and he gave it away to a friend whose wife had lost her own child and now took this one to her breast.

As the dangers of that fateful year thickened and news came of persecutions and massacres, the Church trembled and wondered how she would endure. Finally it became known that Boxers were marching on the village. Mr. Wang was recognised as leader of the local Christians, and to him they would certainly come. He called his little boy and girl to kneel with him in the cave, and committed the matter to God. At sunset, a sound of rushing wind was heard and a violent thunderstorm burst on the district. Hail, wind, and rain were followed by a terrific cloud-burst which swept man and beast away in its irresistible violence. The narrow mountain roads were completely carried away by the course of the waters, and the Boxers never came.

It was a great spiritual experience for Mr. Wang, to whom God spake not in the thunder nor in the storm, but in a still small voice which asserted His boundless claim on the life preserved from danger. From that time he was conscious of a new strength and power, which resulted in his shortly giving up his trade of metal-worker to take charge of the Hwochow Men's Opium Refuge. That position he still holds, and thanks to him the good name and repute of this institution is widespread. All his noblest gifts find their full development in the work which makes hourly claims on patience, forbearance, devotion, long- suffering, meekness, and all those qualities which are bound up in the one characteristic of love. From amongst the men in his charge a steady stream return home to destroy idols and subsequently request baptism. When the question is asked: "How came you to believe?" the answer will be: "I owe it to Pastor Wang, who taught me about Christ and taught me to pray." His methods are not those of the evangelist who gathers in the crowds, but one by one he wins them to the Lord. In one particular only did I hear him censured by a Christian, and that was on the occasion of his ordination to the pastorate. A Church member protested that a stronger man than Wang Bing-guin was needed for the work. "See my case," he said. "When, as you know, I was recently the subject of persecution, I came to Elder Wang for assistance. He listened to my story and urged me to pray and have patience.

"This I did, but matters only got worse, and I returned to insist on his taking action on my behalf. Would you believe that he spoke of nothing more practical than prayer and patience again? On the third occasion, when I had very nearly made up my mind to go straight to the Mandarin, he only urged: 'I fear that prayer and patience are your only lawful weapons, my brother.'"

The opinion of the heathen regarding Mr. Wang was forced upon my attention in a rather startling way. We were preaching one day to a group of village women, and as an old lady in the crowd heard us explaining that "all have sinned and come short of the glory of God," she said: "Those words are untrue, for I knew a man who never spoke a false word and never did an unkind deed." Interested, we asked who he was, and she replied: "Oh, he afterwards followed your Church; his name is Wang Bing-guin."

A VISIT TO THE BASE

"Your heavenly Father knoweth that ye are needing all these things."

"I would be undone if I had not access to the King's chamber of Presence to show Him all the business."— Rutherford.

"Dear children,
  Let us not be loving in word nor yet with the tongue,
  But in deed and truth."

The First Epistle of John.

CHAPTER XIV

A VISIT TO THE BASE

FROM WHENCE WE ARE AGAIN SENT
FORTH WITH FRESH SUPPLIES

I T WAS with mixed feelings that we came to realise that the days were few until that experience known as "taking furlough" was to be ours. It was indeed hard to leave our post. England seemed so far away, and the thought of having to readjust oneself to English ways and

SCRIPTURE TESTIMONY
God's work will not lack God's supply
PHILIPPIANS 4:19

English dress was not inviting. The desire, to see relatives and friends pulled toward the West, but I realised that an even stronger magnet was drawing me with tremendous force to remain in the land of the Celestial.

It was arranged that two experienced missionaries, the Misses Higgs and Johnson, should join Miss Mandeville who had been with us for nearly two years, during our absence. A year of strenuous effort on their part in a post requiring the exercise of tact and forbearance, enabled us to see marked progress in the work upon our return a year later.

In order to carry out our plan of advance new buildings were necessary, and a consultation was held as to the sum required. On the most economical computation this would certainly be £500, and we left for England with the hope and prayer that if it were for the glory of God this sum might be forthcoming.

The months passed by, and sums various were contributed. We were due to leave England in March, and we were still far short of the required amount, when in February, my friend and Pastor, Dr. Campbell Morgan, arranged that I should have an opportunity of telling the members of Westminster Chapel of the work in Hwochow. It was Sunday morning and the usual collection for Church expenses had been taken, but at the close of the service Dr. Morgan announced that those who wished to do so might send contributions to him, which would be forwarded to me. Thanks to the generosity and kindness of those concerned, we left for China with our £500 less £50. In March we started on the interesting journey through Siberia, bringing with us that which was of more value than much gold, Miss French's younger sister, Francesca, to join us in our missionary work.

We reached Moscow, that fascinating city with its churches, Kremlin, and numerous historic interests. We seemed to be at the parting of the way where East and West meet and merge. Partly for the sake of economy and partly for the interest of being more with the people of the land, we, decided to travel, not by the *train de luxe*, but by the Russian daily post train. We were thus able with comfort to do the journey from London to Peking for £20 each, whereas by, the International train £35 is required for fare alone.

How keenly we enjoyed it all! The wide, roomy railway compartments, the slow, steady movement of the broad gauge train, enabling one to read and write with comfort; the rush with a tin kettle for hot water from the huge tanks with unlimited supply, provided at each station; the buying of the day's provision from the peasants who crowded to the platforms with eggs, butter, and milk; the reading aloud of some Russian book in the Slavonic surroundings, which contributed so much to make its disconcerting unexpectednesses seem the natural expression of the Russian temperament.

How delightful it all was; but when we reached Manchuria Town and found ourselves in the midst of Chinese, we felt the thrill which comes with the first sight of home. A few more days, and we were in Peking.

We walked in the acres of parkland which surround the Temple of Heaven, and saw its blue-and-yellow-tiled roofs outlined on the azure of the Eastern sky. We stood in the pavilion where the "Son of Heaven," fasting, rested before he proceeded to pray for his people in the double office of priest and king.

What gorgeous scenes the midnight skies have witnessed where the altar raises its marble carvings and mystic symbols to the open vault of heaven. No sign of idolatry is visible; here he worshipped Heaven and Earth, and bowed before the Supreme Ruler, praying for the millions of his people to whom he stood as father. A magnificent conception! The mind of man could scarcely rise higher in ethics of worship, as in solemn splendour the beasts are slain, and the prostrate Emperor under the starlit sky calls upon the unknown god. Confucius seemed to realise the unbridgable chasm between the offender and his judge when he said: "If a man have offended against heaven, there is none to whom he can pray"; and here the ruler of this great people prayed, but with a recognition of limitation which brought him, later on, back to the familiar idol shrines with an offering of incense and acceptable gifts.

From the quiet dreams of that place, we returned to the hustle and bustle of native city life. Our rickshaw men, with marvellous speed and agility, were soon rushing us through the crowds of pedlars shouting, yelling, and calling on every passer-by to purchase their goods. Beggars, scarcely recognisable as human beings, knocked their foreheads on the ground, beseeching us to give them some cash. The moral support of a policeman is inadequate to the task of protecting the newcomer who has yielded to an impulse of pity.

On we rushed through massive gates, where we ran serious risks of an overturn in meeting a string of heavily laden camels, with sonorous bell hanging to the neck; brightly and gaily dressed ladies passed and repassed in rickshaws; men on horseback, coalheavers, foreign women on bicycles, shining motor-cars, and glass-panelled, silk-upholstered carriages composed a moving picture, with the gates and huge enclosure of the forbidden city as background. From the pandemonium of Chinatown we swung into Legation quarter, where macadamised roads take the place of cobblestones, and for this you call down blessings on civilisation, the rubber tyres of your rickshaw running rapidly and smoothly over the way. Without transition, you pass from East to West. The Wagon-Lits Hotel's fine buildings face you, large foreign shops abound, at night electric lights will blaze over the streets still filled with pleasure-seekers, thoughtless and forgetful, though the words written in days of siege can be clearly descried on the broken fragment of Legation wall: "Lest We Forget."

At the Hongkong and Shanghai Bank we entered to transfer money which was to enable us to erect those longed-for buildings in Hwochow. Whilst I was transacting my business, a voice behind me addressed Miss French by name, and the cashier looked up quickly. Immediately upon the conclusion of my business he asked: "Is that Miss French of Taiyüanfu? Fifty pounds have been lying to her account for three years, and we have been unsuccessful in tracing her whereabouts." Identity having been fully established the money with interest was paid to us, and with our £500 complete and some extra, we journeyed homewards. A strange coincidence you say! Yea, verily, unless "we take our courage in both hands, and call it God."

After a train journey for the next two days, came slow travelling from Taiyüanfu to Hwochow. Long and weary days, in which one takes many hours to accomplish thirty miles, turning in at night to a Shansi inn. A wonderful place it is, carried on with the minimum of expense and trouble to the owner, whose responsibility ends when he has provided you with a kettle of boiling water in an absolutely empty room, the walls and ceiling of which are dirty beyond description. In the courtyard are a few sheds where your mules are stalled for the night, while horses and donkeys, kicking and braying, vie with *insecta* in enlivening for you the hours of darkness. Meanwhile your landlord has sent to ask whether you are requiring food. The bill of fare offers *mien*,[1] with accompanying condiments of salt, vinegar, and red pepper. Should you be a *bon vivant* you will ask for onion and a few bean sprouts, though this entail the reckless expenditure of the further sum of one penny. You lodge a protest at such extortionate charges, for, as your servant remarks, "at such a price we cannot afford to eat." Two

---

1   Vermicelli—cut with a knife.

sticks cut from a tree serve for table cutlery. "I hate luxury," said Goethe, "it kills the imagination." Here imagination flourishes. Through the dirt and grime of the wall I can decipher a poem which tells me that when I come to reckon with my landlord, my account will be as flowing river. Other scrawls eulogise him, and assure me: "Whoever sleeps upon this *kang*, sleeps in peace." (I must have been an exception!) An idol, half-torn, hangs in one corner of the room, and in another I discover a Christian tract. Who has passed this way before me? I am aroused from my reverie by the sound of a voice, which utters, without seeing the humour and pathos of the remark: "The foreign devil is reading characters." I turn to see an eye filling the space of a torn piece of window paper, shamelessly scrutinizing me, and as I do so the intruder withdraws to discuss with the muleteers my failings, virtues, and intimate habits. Long before light the men are calling us, and we arise, anxious to lose none of the cool morning air. Delays occur, for last night a portion of the harness was pawned to pay for the men's supper. Either we supply the necessary money to redeem the pledge, or wait there indefinitely. We first declare that nothing will make us produce that sum which they are not entitled to receive until the journey's end, but both they and we know that a compromise must be effected. Alas, it is already light and the sun rises glorious, but to-day we are to reach home, and nothing seems hard. A short stay for dinner, and at sunset the gates of Hwochow are visible. I cannot describe these homecomings; the welcomers and welcomed know, and that is enough.

THE BUILDERS

"The house is not for me, it is for Him.
His Royal thoughts require many a stair,
Many a tower, many an outlook fair,
Of which I have no thought, and need no care.
Where I am most perplexed, it may be there
Thou makest a secret chamber holy—dim,
Where Thou wilt come to help my deepest prayer."
George Macdonald.

"Toil, workman, toil; thy gracious Lord
Will give thee soon a full reward;
Then toil, obedient to His word,
Until He come.

Sing, pilgrim, sing; Christ's mighty Hand
Will bring thee safe to that bright land;
Then sing—it is thy Lord's command—
Until He come."
Anon.

CHAPTER XV

THE BUILDERS

RELATING HOW THE SUPPLIES WERE USED

I N AN incredibly short space of time our compound was overrun by a gang of one hundred men from the province of Honan. The land in Southern Shansi has been too fertile and yielded too rich a crop of opium to leave us good workmen; when therefore we want work quickly and well done, we inquire for a Honan or Shantung man.

Our helpers searched the countryside for likely trees, which were felled and in a few days made their reappearance as pillars and beams, Old buildings were bought, demolished, and sorted into usable and unusable material, so that as the walls went up the empty spaces about the city increased in number.

Before dawn each morning we were aroused by the beating of a loud gong which called the men to work. This work they might not leave until the last streak of daylight had faded, except for the brief space allowed for breakfast and dinner, when huge cauldrons of a sticky mass of boiled millet was ladled out in generous portions. Millet is the cheapest grain food procurable, and the Shansi man cannot thrive upon it; to the Honan man it is the staff of life, and in consequence their rate of wage is lower.

A race of giants they were, handsome, magnificently built, and well skilled in the use of their simple tools. In the use of the adze they were particularly proficient, and able to plane a section of wood to within a hairbreadth of thickness by the use of this alone. They liked to use it for the most delicate work, so certain are they of their accurate manipulation, and on one occasion when I supplied a bandage to bind a wound on the finger of a workman who had met with a slight accident, as I turned to take up my scissors, the head carpenter, without a trace of humour on his face, stepped forward with a four-foot long adze, and offered to sever the calico.

Heavy work requiring the combined strength of several men, such as the beating in of foundations, or the lifting of a great beam, was accompanied by the sound of the weirdest rhythmic chant, sustained for hours if needs be.

A night watchman was employed, who in accordance with the custom of the country constantly beat a loud gong, by means of which any intending thief is made aware that all are not asleep. The English policeman's rubber sole, and the Chinese watchman's noisy methods, strange to relate, attain the same ends.

On one occasion, hearing blood-curdling yells at midday, we inquired and were told that a workman had caught a tramp, red-handed, in the act of stealing his tools. Our informant described him as aged, starved, and infirm, "truly pitiable," and strung up by his thumbs to a beam. The sound of those yells made us fear that something akin to the famous death by slow degrees, so constantly referred to in Chinese jurisprudence, was being carried into effect at our very door. Pastor Wang, the merciful, was already interceding on the man's behalf, and we sent a peremptory message that the thing must stop. Our desire was acceded to, and the wretched victim made his escape, more terrified than really hurt.

The next reminder of the incident was the following item in the builder's final account: "To missing tools, unclaimed in accordance with missionaries' loving heart, 2s."

One of the minor expenses connected with our building operations was the inviting of guests to a succession of feasts. The occasion of the stamping of the contract in the *Yamen*, which marked the conclusion of the middlemen's responsibility in the purchase of property, was celebrated by a handsome meal, to which all in any way connected with the transaction were invited.

The necessity of conciliating our neighbours to the inevitable trouble which the dust and litter of building would entail upon them, caused us to spread another feast, to which all who could shelter beneath the term "neighbour" were asked.

By the building contract we found ourselves obliged to conform to the customary requirement made by workmen that every tenth day we should provide a "reward for work," which, in fact, amounted to supplying one pound of white flour and a handful of vegetable to each workman.

This arrangement ensured pleasant relations between the men and ourselves, for each time they were our guests grievances were forgotten and a fresh start made. The swinging of the huge beams of the church roof was the occasion for extra festivity.

This custom of inviting guests does much to smooth over difficulties, and is customary, not only in matters of building, but also on numerous other occasions. For instance, the autumn rains swelling the river necessitate the use of a ferry boat for about two months of the year. The expense of this is met by public subscriptions from the more important people of the city, and a small fare for each passenger. Those whose names appear on the subscription list are invited to an annual banquet given by the ferrymen; I have often wondered what would happen were some simple soul to accept the invitation, which in reality is only intended to serve as a reminder that subscriptions are now due.

It is part of the convenient social system of this land that no woman would presume to put in an appearance on such occasions. Throughout the building operations the only part of the feast in which we were privileged to share—which privilege was unquestioningly granted—was the payment of all expenses.

How glad we should have been to find such an easy solution to the problem of the importunate widow. This aged lady entered a claim for two stones occupying nine square feet of waste land, to the sale of which she declared her consent had never been given. The matter had been referred to middlemen who decided in our favour; nevertheless, we learned to dread the daily tap, tap, of her stick, and the shrill squawk of her strident voice as she came with fresh deeds (some of them dating back to former dynasties) of which she demanded the examination. She was generally accompanied by friends, all of whom were prepared to support her claim.

I have seen her stand by the workmen, and with her nagging tongue drive them, and the foreman, almost to despair. It was impossible to recognise her rights even to the extent of feasting her, so we endured until the walls were built, and then to compensate her for her trouble handed her the equivalent of 2s., which sum she accepted, but every time we meet her she reminds us that we are occupying land which belongs to her.

The first autumn frosts saw a large expanse of waste land, which had formerly lain around our compound, transformed into a neat series of courtyards, and a spacious church occupied seventy feet of the main street frontage, providing sitting accommodation for a congregation of six hundred. In all, we had erected fifty *gien*[1] of room space, in addition to the church.

Thanks to an unusually profitable rate of silver exchange which held during these few months, and owing to the faithful oversight and scrupulous economy of Pastor Wang and his helpers, our £500 proved sufficient to meet all necessary requirements of Church, School, Bible School, and Dispensary.

---

1   The space between two beams in a Chinese building.

WOMEN'S BIBLE TRAINING SCHOOL

"Woe is me if I preach not the Gospel."

Motto of the Hwochow Bible School.

"Cornelius halted at a doorway in a long, low wall—the outer wall of some villa courtyard, it might be supposed— as if at liberty to enter, and rest there awhile. He held the door open for his companion to enter also, if he would, with an expression, as he lifted the latch, which seemed to ask Marius, "Would you like to see it?" Was he willing to look upon that, the seeing of which might define—yes! define the critical turning-point in his days?"—Walter Pater.

CHAPTER XVI

WOMEN'S BIBLE TRAINING SCHOOL

WHICH TELLS HOW A LINK WAS ESTABLISHED BETWEEN WESTMINSTER AND HWOCHOW BIBLE SCHOOLS

A MONGST THE courtyards which constituted our new premises was one into the walls of which was inserted a stone, engraved with the words in Chinese and English: "Women's Bible School. Erected by the Congregation of Westminster Chapel, London. Jesus said: 'I am the Way, the Truth, and the Life.'"

The women's rooms had never been large enough to hold those who were anxious to come, and now at last suitable premises were going to make possible the fulfilment of a long-cherished plan—that of giving adequate training to suitable women.

It seemed a long step from the days when, freely roaming around the villages, we taught some of these women the very first character they knew, spelling out with them the text: "God so loved the world that He gave His only-begotten Son, that whosoever believeth in Him should not perish, but have everlasting life." The next step had been attendance at a station class for twenty days, sometimes repeated yearly but never leading to advanced work. In our new premises we divided the students into three groups: Firstly, those attending a ten days' course, who served as training-ground to a second group of more advanced women who had passed the initial stage, and who now entered for the two years' course of Bible training and practical experience as evangelists. Thirdly, a picked few who, having received more regular teaching, were able to continue their own studies and help to superintend the work of the juniors, especially on the practical side, meanwhile giving a considerable portion of their time to aggressive evangelistic work.

Foremost amongst these was Mrs. Liang, mother of Ling Ai, the head-mistress of the girls' school. Strong, true, a woman of no ordinary ability, little escaped her penetrating glance. It was in middle age that she first heard the Gospel, an indirect influence of the opium refuge work; for Mrs. Liang had never smoked opium, nor had any member of her family. A neighbour, however, had, and on her return from the Refuge she produced with pardonable pride the copy of St. John's Gospel which she had bought, and better still, could read. It was hard for Mrs. Liang to see the former degraded opium smoker ahead of her in learning, and she persuaded her husband to give her the needed help. She borrowed the book and started at the first chapter. She had not been to the Mission House nor had she seen the missionaries, but before she met them she had met their Lord. It was but one more proof that "the words I speak unto you they are spirit, and they are life," and the Holy Spirit illuminating the written pages brought home to her its meaning. "He came unto His own, and His own received Him not," she read, and how can I say what took place? She tells me that she was convicted of sin, and that she found her Saviour.

Intercourse with Miss Jacobsen was soon established, and under Mr. Cheng's influence her husband also believed. Mrs. Liang was baptized, her own feet and Ling Ai's were unbound, and the latter became a pupil in the girls' school.

Mrs. Liang herself lived quietly at home until the year 1900. At that time the local Boxer leader was a near neighbour of hers, and he was prepared to kill these well-known adherents of a foreign religion. On recovering consciousness, however, from the trance which preceded the issuing of inspired orders, he uttered the surprising words: "Return each to your own place; let each busy himself with his own affairs." Not daring to disobey his followers scattered, and the small group of Christians was safe. Ling Ai has described the experiences of those days in the following words: "For months we were as those whose hair is bound around the neck, not knowing at what moment we should be called upon to die, but after our deliverance we united in saying: 'We have been under the shadow of the Almighty.'"

When we came to Hwochow Mrs. Liang, realising our difficulties, was one of the first to come to our assistance, and quickly endeared herself to us by her thoughtful, kind, practical ways.

To the work of preaching she gave herself with unusual energy and devotion, so that to-day there are few women in Hwochow who do not know her, and scarcely a courtyard that has not been visited by her.

Assisting Mrs. Liang is Mrs. Bah, who the first time I saw her refused to have any intercourse with us. She was the senior wife; of a wealthy man who had died early, leaving the two widows to arrange matters as best they could. The younger one smoked opium, but was the proud possessor of a son who by law was the property of the elder wife, but it was obvious that to the younger was due the honour of introducing a son and heir to the house.

The fact that Mrs. Bah the younger at last became a Christian and left her evil habits, did not make the elder woman more friendly, though she had in time to confess that life was easier for both under the new conditions. After some time the Christians of the village received her permission to use a cave in her spacious court for worship, in return for their offer to put it in repair. "It can do no harm," she argued, "and repairs are badly needed." Every evening they met to read the Bible and pray, and Mrs. Bah, prompted by curiosity, took her spinning to within earshot. She understood little, but the reiteration of the words "Heavenly Father" puzzled and interested her. "If it really be the Heavenly Father whom they worship," she reasoned, "they should be in the best room." The thought grew upon her until a change was effected, and to this day Mrs. Bah's guest-room is the village church. She soon left her spinning-wheel to join the worshippers and gradually came to the triumphant belief, weak at first, but taking slow shape, that "the attitude of the soul to its Maker can be something more than a distant reverence and overpowering awe, that we can indeed hold converse with God, speak with Him, call upon Him, put—to use a human phrase—our hand in His, desiring only to be led according to His will." This was the spiritual story of Mrs. Bah.

I could tell of many others and the theme is tempting, for by so many and such varied paths have these comrades travelled. To mention only our youngest student who at the age of sixteen, member of a heathen family, heard the Gospel of Jesus Christ from an elder sister, a patient of the Women's Opium Refuge. She determined that as far as in her lay she would be a Christian. Yielding to her wishes, her parents engaged her to the son of a believer. After her marriage, when her entrance to the Bible School was suggested we demurred, but agreed to her attending a station class, only to discover that once more the Spirit of God had accomplished that of which we knew nothing. This young woman, who had only heard the Gospel from a sister who herself did not believe, had been truly converted. Reference to the curriculum in Appendix A will make it clear that the subject which has the pre-eminence is Bible study. The students prepare the books there mentioned, and during the years they are with us cover also the course indicated by Dr. Campbell Morgan's Graded Bible, which Miss French has translated for their use.

The instruction of inquirers in the village centres is undertaken by those women evangelists who have completed their course. In places to which they are invited by the local church they hold classes of ten days' duration, following the course of study as in the central station. By this means a large number of women are under instruction, and heathens are brought in contact with the messengers of the Cross.

City and village visiting forms an important branch of the training, and last but not least, classes taken under criticism, when it falls to the lot of the missionary to ask the questions which might occur to a heathen audience, and to impress upon the students the necessity of clear presentation of the Gospel. It is desirable that they should express the things which have gripped them in an individual way, not adopting a Western colouring but using to the full their Eastern knowledge: "Originality is like a fountain head; orthodoxy is too often only the unimpeachable fluid of the water company."

The prodigal son, for example, naturally smoked opium in the far country, and the Chinese pictures so represent him. It was not, as we have supposed, in her confidence that oil would be supplied that the widow's faith was exemplified, but rather in her willingness at Elisha's command to go forth on a borrowing expedition when she was already so deeply in debt.

We are sometimes treated to illustrations truly Eastern in character, as the following example will indicate. It was accepted by the audience as a solemn exhortation, as was the preacher's intention, the missionaries being the only ones present to whom the humorous side was evident. The subject was the importance of a whole hearted acceptance of the Gospel, and the foolishness and uselessness of a half-hearted belief. A man, we were told, was begging by the roadside; he was very ill, and a passing doctor had pity on him, and gave him some medicine which the man promised to take. Questionings, however, arose in his mind as to the reliability of the said doctor, and yet he could not but take the drug, as he felt so ill. A compromise was decided upon, and he took half the dose. For a few hours he felt wonderfully well, and rejoiced in his restored condition; towards night the pain was more acute than before, and he was at his wits' end. How he regretted his folly, for his illness was certainly more serious. A few months later the same doctor, travelling over the same road, met the same man now reduced to a bag of bones.

"What!" said he; "are you not the man to whom I gave medicine last time I came this way?" "I am," he replied, "and I have been much worse ever since."

"Worse!" exclaimed the physician; "how is that?"

"I only took half the dose," said the man; "I did not venture to take the whole."

"Alas! alas!" he replied, "how terrible! Your illness is the result of parasites attacking your vitals. That medicine would have killed them all. Had you taken the full dose you would have been well; had you tasted none there would have been hope for you. You took a small dose, and the parasites were sent to sleep, and later, when the effect of the drug had gone over, they awoke more lively than ever. Having once tasted of the drug and experienced its effect, nothing will induce them to be trapped a second time. Return home, and prepare for a lingering death."

In the moral drawn, the folly of an endeavour to serve two masters was made clear—a truth which all present felt to have been powerfully interpreted.

THE DRAW NET LET DOWN INTO THE SEA

Take up God's inspired word anywhere you like, and while we are called upon to adore the sovereign counsel of God and to say constantly that it transcends and surpasses all that we can do and all that we can expect, yet He does not bring the season of refreshing without engaging His children to help Him. The splendour of the grace may sometimes conceal man's effort, but it never cancels it."—Rev. Elvit Lewis.

CHAPTER XVII

THE DRAW NET LET DOWN INTO THE SEA

AN ACCOUNT OF FRESH EFFORTS TO REACH THE
MULTITUDE AND BRING THEM TO DECISION

ETHODS IN mission work are many, and the diversities of gifts bestowed by the one Spirit are manifest in the striking variety of means put forth to bring to a knowledge of Christ the people of the lands in which the members of His Church are called to work.

The teacher rejoices to see the change brought about by discipline and regular life in those committed to his care. The doctor, exercising his gift, succeeds where others have failed in establishing confidence and friendly relations which prepare a road for those who follow. The itinerant missionary sacrifices the comfort of a settled dwelling to carry the Gospel to those who dwell outside the radius touched by the central station.

By the exercise of his peculiar gift, each expresses the longing that in the hearts of the people he sees around, without God and without hope, may take place that greatest of miracles called conversion. Nevertheless, every missionary has ever to guard against a most subtle and deadening influence which may be likened to poisonous gas in the enemy's country, lulling him to a condition wherein the idolatrous practices of the people around, instead of stirring him to greater activity, come to be regarded as customs of the nations amongst whom he lives, deplorable but interesting practices.

The horror experienced on first seeing men bow down to wood and stone may give way to a complacency which ceases to expect an immediate response to the quickening and convicting power of the Spirit of God, and philosophises on the gradual emergence of light from the kingdom of darkness. The deadening of that vitality which drives a man to the seeking of the lost is one of the master-strokes of the enemy of souls, and one which no man doing spiritual work can afford to ignore.

The sense of this urgency, and a great desire that our Chinese fellow-workers might realise the fulness of their vocation as evangelists, emboldened us to move in what was then a somewhat new direction so far as North China was concerned, by the holding of a six days' Mission for women in our new church in the spring after its dedication.

Miss Gregg of Hwailu, in the Province of Chihli, when travelling through Shansi some years previously had conducted meetings for school-girls in several stations, upon which the blessing of God manifestly rested. From that time plans were being matured in the minds of the missionaries at Hwochow for a Mission to women in that city at the earliest possible date. The erection of a church building which could hold the number expected made that dream a possibility. The city and villages were visited by the women evangelists, placards were posted on the walls, and every effort was made to widely advertise. Prayer was offered throughout the Church that God would so prevent us in all our doings that we might see His salvation.

The men gladly undertook the arrangements for catering, made necessary by the fact that women cannot go to the shops to buy food for themselves, and this department was splendidly managed. We prepared to receive three hundred guests, and about three hundred and fifty took advantage of the invitation, who, with schoolgirls, Bible School students and helpers, provided a resident congregation of little short of five hundred. They came long distances on donkey-back, in carts, or even walking many miles.

Large numbers of heathen, attracted by the unique sight of so large a concourse of women, swelled the numbers at the daily evangelistic meetings, and it was an inspiration to see the new church packed with women and girls quietly and reverently listening to the Gospel message. A room was set apart where silence was observed, that those who wished to do so might pray without fear of disturbance. A band of helpers was appointed to teach the passage for the day, and outside the church in an adjoining court was a book-stall, and here a brisk trade was done in hymn-sheets, gospels, and block-printed texts.

The elder scholars, anxious to do their part, acted as stewards; each one had charge of some part of the building, so that should a baby cry and threaten to divert attention, she could carry the small offender to an adjoining room and keep it there until such time as it was prepared to enjoy the larger gathering. One of the "old girls" took charge of small children, and managed her creche so successfully that we were undisturbed by the younger portion of the community.

Each morning before seven a gong sounded and all assembled for prayer. After breakfast a short Bible-reading was given, the subject chosen being the sevenfold "I Am" of St. John's Gospel. These meetings were simple and evangelistic, and many testified to blessing received as they saw afresh all the wealth laid up in Him who is the Way, the Truth, and the Life.

It was to the eleven and four o'clock meetings that the crowds gathered. While the congregation was assembling a choir of schoolgirls sang hymns, and after reading of Scripture and prayer by a Chinese lady, the address was given by Miss Gregg. The women listened intently as she talked, and illustrated her remarks by objects so familiar. The fan used for winnowing the grain is, I think, now never used by those who attended without the thought asserting itself afresh that thus He will separate the wheat from the chaff.

This Mission accomplished all that we had hoped. Christ the Redeemer was revealed to some who, in obedience to the wishes of the head of their household, had passively substituted Christianity for that system of idolatrous observances which had constituted their religious life.

Christ the Master laid His claim upon some who had believed, but never served.

Even heathen women, listening to the earnest, convincing words, were startled to a realisation that the offer of salvation with which they were faced compelled a decision on one side or the other, that the detached view with which they had hitherto regarded Christianity could no longer be maintained. Amongst the schoolgirls were some, daughters of Christians, who were in precisely the same position as girls in a homeland; They neither doubted nor questioned, but they now realised that the whole matter had assumed a personal aspect, and the individual spirit was summoned to an audience with its Maker.

The Evangelists, Bible women, and ripe Christians amongst us suddenly saw the fields white, and every dilatory thought which suggested the perennial excuse: "There are yet four months and then cometh the harvest," was silenced in a sense of immediate urgency: "I must be about my Master's business." This gathering affected a wide area, for our visitors came from the counties of Hungtung, Chaocheng, and Fensi, now all gladly welcomed by the Hwochow church, and missionaries from those districts came to share with us in the campaign.

*   *   *   *   *   *   *   *   *

Six years have passed, and once more a Mission for women is advertised to be held on the occasion of an idol procession which brings thousands into town from the neighbouring villages. This time our own evangelistic band was sufficiently strong to undertake the speaking to an audience almost entirely composed of heathen, who now heard, not from a foreigner, but from their own people, of the Truth as it is in Jesus. Once more we saw decisions made and the evidence of the working of God's Spirit.

Thus was a further step taken in aggressive work amongst the women, and a further impetus given to the self-propagation of the Gospel, and to the fulfilment of the prophecy of Pastor Hsi that even Hwochow should see a Resurrection morning.

LIFE AMONGST THE UPPER TEN THOUSAND

"Is it not delightful to have friends coming from distant quarters"
Confucius.

"All within the four seas are brethren."
Confucius.

"Society and solitude are deceptive names. It is not the circumstance of seeing more or fewer people, but the readiness of sympathy, that imports."—Emerson.

CHAPTER XVIII

LIFE AMONGST THE UPPER TEN THOUSAND

RECORDING HOSPITALITY SHOWN TO
US BY THE OFFICIAL CLASSES-

IN THE centre of every Chinese city stands the *Yamen*, where resides the Mandarin, addressed as "Father of the people," before whom their wrongs must be laid, and who, as direct representative of the central Government, exercises autocratic power. His word is law, a man must kneel in his presence when addressing him, and it is a penal offence to enter his private dwelling-court unsummoned. His term of office is limited to a few years, and a change of official entails the removal of his whole suite. The new Mandarin will bring with him his secretaries, underlings, men and women servants, and the prosperity of a city will largely depend upon the personal attitude of the "Great Man" to matters of reform.

Our intercourse with the Hwochow *Yamen* has been frequent, and owing to the strong attitude taken by the leaders of the Church against interference in law cases where Christians are concerned, it has been of a purely social character.

My first visit was in answer to a request from the Mandarin that I would go to see his wife who was suffering from acute toothache. I was requested to make preparations for an extraction, and was informed that if it suited my convenience I should be fetched that same afternoon. Accordingly, I made ready and in due course the Yamen carriage arrived, a springless, but elegantly upholstered cart, and accompanied by a woman servant we started. Ahead of us an outrider, dressed in a long gown, wore a hat of the inverted bowl shape, decorated with a spreading scarlet tassel. Behind followed other retainers, and thus escorted we passed in triumphal procession through the quiet Hwochow streets. After many bumps and anxious moments as we splashed in and out of mud-pits, we turned into the wide space which surrounds the outermost entrance of the Yamen. Here crowds of men were reading the latest proclamation pasted to the walls, whilst others, talking earnestly, discussed the case tried that very day, of the poor man who in vain sought redress from the rapacity of his wealthy neighbour. He had knelt, and laying his forehead to the ground at the feet of the Mandarin pleaded for justice, but only to find that his condemnation was a foregone conclusion. All these groups were scattered by the yells of our outrider and the cracks of our carter's whip, and the sellers of cooked food gathered their piles of little bowls and swiftly set them out of harm's way, for the habits of Yamen retainers are well known to the populace, and there is little satisfaction to be had when complaints are presented and compensation for destroyed goods is claimed. With ever-increasing speed and corresponding agony, we were driven up the steep ascent which leads to the outer courtyard, where after a preliminary bump down two steps we found ourselves on comparatively smooth ground, and rolled along a broad, high, paved path leading to the second great archway where our conveyance came to a standstill, and we waited whilst our cards were taken and presented to the ladies we had come to see. Many soldiers were standing about, and various instruments used in the punishment of prisoners were fastened to the walls as warning to all who passed, that way. A very few minutes and we were invited to leave our cart and follow the man appointed to conduct us to the innermost court where the *Tai-tais*[1] lived; slaves attended us on either side, whilst the retainer went ahead carrying our scarlet cards breast high before him.

---

1   The polite term for the wife of an official.

A vista of courtyards opened one from another, and we saw a number of little ladies in charming, brilliant, butterfly-like garments coming to meet us with odd, graceful, stilted movements. Everything must from this point be done according to the strictest etiquette, so the *Tai-tai* of least rank came first to meet us, and led us back to where stood the head wife, in whose presence we respectfully removed our eyeglasses and made a bow.

There were a large number of women about, for this Mandarin had two wives besides several daughters-in-law. We were invited to a reception room where carpets, felts, tables, and chairs were all scarlet in colour, and here were served with delicious fragrant tea and small cakes, in which were mixed rose leaves, nuts, and sugar. All the preliminary questions required by good manners were first asked—our respective "venerable ages" and details of our various near relatives—but soon curiosity overflowed into many inquiries concerning our "honourable country," and we were helped to more tea and cakes, and begged to make ourselves at home. We, on our part, led the conversation back to matters concerned with the object of our residence in this country, and received from our hostess extravagant compliments upon our extraordinary ability and learning, the reputation of which, they said, was well known to the Mandarin.

The object of my visit was then mentioned, and I was asked to see the tooth, of which, being very loose, I recommended the extraction, and was able to assure the patient that the pain would not be very great. Many of the younger women gathered around her, comforting her, and covered her eyes that she might not see the forceps; they begged her to remember that the pain would soon be over, and as soon as I could induce her to open her mouth, I removed the troublesome member. "How wonderful!" they all exclaimed. "Why, it did not hurt at all!"

After such a surgical triumph, long-neglected and half-forgotten pains were remembered by the bystanders, and all the ladies on my next visit came to me with some complaint. We sought to awaken in them the sense of those far deeper ills which they so little realised, finding once more that in following the method of Christ a sense of need had been awakened: "Ye seek Me because ye did eat of the loaves and were filled. I am the bread of life."

As soon as the operation was over, we suggested that we must be returning home, but this could not be allowed until we had partaken of further refreshment, and servants appeared with delicacies —meat balls in gravy, flavoured as only a Chinese cook can flavour, lotus seeds in syrup, luscious fruits, sweetmeats, and a drink of apricot kernels, sweet to excess. The meat balls were daintily wrapped in pastry, and as she helped me to some of these, the *Tai-tai* said: "I think you do not care for pork." I replied that we did not as a rule eat much pork. "I am so glad," she said; "these are fowl, and therefore you can eat them without fear." A few days later we heard that the head cook was under severe punishment and incarcerated in a dungeon, because he had not taken the trouble to find out what were our special tastes in matters of the table, and had served pork in place of fowl! Some years later he was a patient in our Refuge, and told Mr. Wang that he would like to make a feast for us. We thought this extremely kind of him, considering what he had suffered on our behalf, and he was asked to our kitchen to prepare the food, while we invited some friends to share it with us. I think he was a man of preconceived ideas rather than a genius at making inquiries, whatever his talent in the culinary art, for he said he knew foreigners liked sweet things, and he served us twenty or more courses of the sweetest food it has been my good fortune to eat.

Our visit proved to be the commencement of a most friendly intercourse. A few days later the outrider, cart, and retainers were at our door again, this time escorting the ladies who had come to return the call. They enjoyed the outing considerably, as is easy to see they would, when one remembers that they had lived three years in Hwochow and had now crossed the threshold of their home for the first time during that period. They could have no intercourse at all with the bourgeoisie of the town, and apart from visitors staying at the *Yamen*, enjoyed no social life.

In due course we were invited to an "eight times eight" feast, consisting of elaborate courses, in which the sweet, the fishy, and the meaty alternated in bewildering miscellany, whilst our vision was delighted by the elegant dishes, the lovely coral china, the pure form of the many-branched candlesticks, and, above all, the graceful, gay little ladies who manipulated the difficult, slippery food with such a masterly command of their nimble chop-sticks. Here for the first time I tasted the delicious birds'-nest soup, gelatinous in consistency and fishy in taste, being, in fact, a mass compounded of seaweed and small fish into a nest by a sea-bird.

So far all was well, but we came home faced by the difficulty that it was now our turn to offer a return feast which must be equally elegant. There was only one cook in the city who was capable of the preparation of a suitable repast, and he was in their employ, and though some surprising things are possible in China, we did not see how we could secure his services to cook a meal for his own mistress. We were, therefore, thrown back upon our slender resources, and decided that an English dinner-party was the only possible solution of the problem. Here at least we were treading upon familiar ground, and were free from the snares of Chinese etiquette. We need have no fear of giving offence to our guests by placing the fish upon the table with its head toward that quarter which would indicate their position to be of military instead of civil rank, and many other equally subtle and delicate questions would now have no terrors for us. We felt it incumbent upon us to do all in our power to please the eye as well as the palate, and while we fully realised our inability to delight our guests with such beauty as that to which they were accustomed, we did our best. Salmon is a great asset, being decorative as well as tasty, and only the hard-pressed know the many uses of a tin of sardines. Jelly is a certain success, and the last plum-pudding from home, cut into dice and blazing in a blue flame, looks mysteriously clever. A bottle of cochineal is worth its weight in gold on such occasions, and the *pièce montée,* which none but an expert could have recognised as spinach, beetroot, carrot, and yam tinted pink, would have done no discredit to Benoist. The novelty of handling spoon and fork, and even so dangerous a weapon as a knife, did much to enhance the pleasure of the meal.

The conversation was now much more intimate than on the earlier occasions, and both sides felt free to ask questions on matters which had excited curiosity. "Does the sun ever shine in your country?" asked the *Tai-tai.* "I have heard that England is a land of shades." "When I left my home in Szechwan I was very homesick. Are you?" inquired another lady, but before I could reply, her companion answered for me: "The ability of these ladies is so great that they would be incapable of such feelings." A guest of their own, who had spent much time in Shanghai, was thoroughly conversant with foreign dress and manners; she described the former with great originality, but admitted that even she was baffled by one thing: "The spotted webbing with which foreign ladies cover their face, is it worn for purposes of concealment or as an aid to the eyesight?" My answer that it served to keep the hair in place carried no conviction, for she had already remarked that though combs are so much in evidence in the foreign woman's coiffure, she seemingly makes little use of them!

The conversation turned to the subject of a proclamation recently issued which forbade the binding of children's feet: "Alas, the people of China are not so easily governed as those of your honourable country," lamented the chief *Tai-tai*. "The Mandarin finds it impossible to enforce this one order, whilst he read in last week's paper that in England a man is imprisoned for refusing to send his child to school, for omitting to vaccinate it, and the article even stated that a parent is punished for refusing to call a doctor to see a sick child, even if it be a girl; but the newspapers are full of fabulous tales!"

SCRIPTURE TESTIMONY
Discernment required to prevent onlookers from stumbling
I CORINTHIANS 8:1-11:1 · I CORINTHIANS 8:7-11 · I CORINTHIANS 9:13 · I CORINTHIANS 10:23-11:1

The next few months saw a growing intimacy and a constant exchange of presents. We were often able to indulge in the famous delicacy of buried eggs, of which the not unpleasant, slightly ammoniated flavour is so much appreciated by the Chinese. Once we were faced by a real difficulty on the occasion of receiving a present of meat, when conscientious Mr. Fu, fearful lest we should shelter under a liberty of conscience whereby we would eat and ask no question, hastily came to warn us that this had been offered to idols before being presented to us. Under these circumstances we had no option but to crave leave to refuse a present whereby a brother might have been caused to stumble.

How little we dreamed of the trouble which would so soon break over the official classes with the overthrow of the Empire, and the establishment of a Republic. I remember the last visit we paid to those friends, and our departure from the *Yamen* in the brilliant moonlight, whilst huge lanterns lighted our path through the archways and great gateways. As we left the huge enclosure the guard fired the first night watch. "Except the Lord keep the city the watchman watcheth but in vain." That night the Revolution broke out in Hankow, and the next time we saw our hostesses they were in terrible distress, imploring our permission to make our house their shelter, should the hatred of the mob break forth and their residence be rioted. They were in a most defenceless position, for the Mandarin had taken a journey to Taiyüanfu, and did not return. He was one of the old school, and faithful to the traditions of the Manchus whose court he had accompanied to Sianfu in the flight of 1900. It was still far from certain which party would gain the ascendancy, and he, as most of his class, wished to refrain from an expression of opinion until the situation was clearly defined. This, however, was not allowed, and during the massacres of the Manchus in Taiyüanfu he was arrested, and made to declare himself.

He held the Hanlin degree, the highest honour to which the Chinese scholar is admitted, the Emperor himself conducting the examinations. Faced by his enemies and fearing summary execution, he sheltered himself behind the agelong reverence for scholarship which exists in China as in no other country: "Death has no terrors for me," he calmly said, "but, alas, that such a scholar should be lost to China!" No armed bodyguard could have afforded him such protection as this transference of insult from his own person to the learning he represented. No man present was prepared to strike a blow at the embodiment of the Divine Right of Scholarship.

He lived to return to Hwochow, where he faced death a second time and was dragged through the streets by an angry populace, but finally escaped and with his wives reached a place of safety.

THE REVOLUTION OF 1911

"For an event to be great, two things must be united— the lofty sentiment of those who accomplish it, and the lofty sentiment of those who witness it. No event is great in itself, even though it be the disappearance of whole constellations, the destruction of several nations, the establishment of vast empires, or the prosecution of wars at the cost of enormous forces: over things of this sort the breath of history blows as if they were flocks of wool. . . . Hence the anxiety which every one must feel who, observing the approach of an event, wonders whether those about to witness it will be worthy of it."—F. Nietzsche.

CHAPTER XIX

THE REVOLUTION OF 1911

AND HOW WE WERE AFFECTED BY IT

THE REVOLUTION of 1911 burst on us like a bolt from the blue. One day we were mildly interested at the signs of trouble in far-removed provinces, and the next, the thing was in our very midst. The first intimation of local disturbance met me in the shape of a contingent of men, parents of some of my scholars, who were introduced to my presence with the startling information that they had come to fetch away their daughters, not daring to leave them in a marked place such as the girls' school would inevitably be, and afraid to delay, lest roads should become so dangerous that their removal would be impossible. I had no option but to agree, and at earliest dawn the next day a few carts and a string of donkeys conveyed them from a side door as quietly and unobtrusively as possible.

Two days later the news of a massacre of the Manchu population of Taiyüanfu reached us; and in accordance with the request of the parents, we hastily scattered all the remaining pupils whose homes were nearer at hand, and the whole city yielded itself to a condition of panic when every wild report was spread and believed.

The little group of foreigners in this town is popularly supposed to have access to the most far-reaching sources of information on matters national and international; therefore when we saw fit to scatter our resident pupils to their homes, the city concluded that secret information had been conveyed to us of trouble ahead. That same night, whilst we slept peacefully in our beds, terror so seized the populace that every young woman who had a village home to which she could withdraw, fled to it. Where horse or donkey was not available they escaped on foot, carrying the bundle which held their clothes, and the gates being shut at dark, numbers climbed down the steep incline of the city wall rather than risk the dangers which they feared might threaten them in the town.

Certainly an anxious time was ahead for all of us. Postal service was interrupted, and we were completely cut off from intercourse by post or telegraph with the outer world. It was uncertain whether the movement would declare itself anti-foreign or anti-Christian, anti-dynastic or anti-Republican. Such uncertainty was felt on this latter political point, that it was a difficult time indeed for the large number whose plain object was to be on the winning side, whichever it might be. Even the commander of the military forces, sent to restore peace in a neighbouring city, provided himself with the badge of either party, that he might, at the city gate, affix that which was representative of the predominant feeling.

The Chinaman has for so long held the view that politics are no individual concern of his, seeing that statesmen are paid to give their time and brains to the consideration of such questions, that it would seem unnatural to be expected to have an opinion on such a technical matter as to whether the Government of the land should remain Imperial or become Republican.

On our compound were collected seven foreign women and about a dozen Chinese girls whose homes were in distant towns, varying from the borders of Mongolia in the north to places twelve days' journey by road in the south.

Much anxious thought was devoted to the question of how the various members of our community could be placed in safe keeping, should it become imperative for us to leave the place.

Finally, Sir John Jordan's recall of all British women and children reached us, and feeling it our duty to obey orders, we hastily boarded a few girls in suitable Christian homes, and left with the others by the North road. A long line of nine litters swung through the great archways of the city gates, soon after dawn on 4th December 1911, to convey us to our nearest point on the railway line, five days' journey away, passing *en route* through a city where we knew that a trustworthy Christian family would take charge, *pro tem*, of some of our Chinese girls.

It was with relief that we saw the distant railway embankment, which indicated to us that we had reached the end of our litter journey, and might now expect to be shortly whirled back to the midst of Western civilisation.

The time-table indicated 9 a.m. as the hour of departure for the morning train, and long ere this our shivering group assembled on the bleak platform. We were evidently not to be kept waiting, for the train stood ready on a siding, and our slight baggage was soon placed in the racks of the only third-class carriage attached to a goods train. Those who have spent years away from the sight of a train will understand the sense of luxury with which we seated ourselves, and waited to hear the whistle which would be the sign of our departure, and feel the swift, easy movement which would carry us over so many miles of road almost without a trace of weariness. Our number had increased to about twenty foreigners, assembled in response to Sir John Jordan's command from various stations, and pleasant conversation so engaged the time that impatience was under control, even though the sun was high in the heavens and still the train was stationary. Our servants, who had heard much of the marvels of steam-engines, still sat on patient heels at the edge of the platform; but doubt of the superiority of this Western notion gained on their minds as the sun passed the meridian and they, with twelve miles to walk for their night's lodging, left us still standing motionless. "A train is a handsome thing to look at, and the amount of iron used in its manufacture must be immense, but for practical purposes give me a cart," was the report they brought home to inquiring friends at Hwochow. In the afternoon we steamed away, under escort of a young man who had just been appointed Secretary of the Foreign Office in the provincial capital by the new revolutionary party. His qualifications for the post consisted chiefly in the fact that, having been employed by a foreign firm as piano-tuner, he could make himself understood in the English tongue on simple subjects.

As far as the station of Yangchuen all went well, but here fresh delay and the unwelcome announcement from our escort that a battle was in progress farther down the line, the metals were required for the conveyance of soldiers, and he must beg of us to make ourselves as comfortable as possible for the night in our compartment. Protest was useless, and we had to submit to see the engine detached and ourselves abandoned, a useless derelict, on a rusty siding. The Secretary of the Foreign Office supplied us with hard-boiled eggs and biscuits, and made his exit, leaving in charge of the gentlemen of the party a packet of silver which he begged might be handed to his mother. By morning stationmaster, guards, porters, and clerks had all vanished from the scene, for the news had come of a reverse to the Revolutionary forces.

Four days and nights we stuck to our third-class carriage and our siding; for part of the time, trains thundered past carrying men to the front, and we were informed that the famous regiment called "Dare-to-die" had gone to crush the Imperial troops. With a thrill we saw these brave warriors pass, but a brief period sufficed to dispel "the great illusion," and twelve hours later the same men were dashing back to Taiyüanfu, carrying a terrible tale. "Had we stayed longer we should have been dead men; the bullets were falling in our midst." The officer, however, gave a different explanation of their return. "Poor chaps, they are worn out, and I must take them back to get a night's rest," he said. No one cared for our plight, as cold, hungry, and deserted we watched the weary day pass to night, and the yet more weary night give place to a dreary dawn. Such experiences are not to be desired, for they who know China best, and the anti-foreign feeling which may at any time manifest itself, are aware how quickly such a position may become critical.

One thing only besides our miserable carriage had been left on the line, and that was three trolleys. The hour dawned on the fourth day when our exhausted patience refused further service, and we determined those trolleys should be made to carry us and our goods to some inhabited region, be it friendly or inimical. That day and the next we spent racing down and crawling up the gradients of the line to Niangtzekwan. The "Dare-todies" boasted of having mined the line, and this did not conduce to ease of mind in being the first to travel over it, especially when we rushed through long tunnels. The line is one which taxed the ingenuity of engineers to the utmost in its construction, and is one succession of light bridges spanning deep chasms, tunnels, and long gradients. Luckily for us, we were travelling in the downhill direction, else our journey had been impossible. If the brave "Dare-to-dies" were too hurried to leave the line mined, they had taken time to destroy it in some places, and once a broken-down engine blocked our path.

The fleeing soldiers had found the engine-driver preparing to take in water, but they would have none of his lagging ways, and compelling him to drive ahead, were soon forced to abandon the useless locomotive. Each such obstacle was a lengthy hindrance, and the kind gentlemen of our party were obliged to organise a breakdown gang to overcome the difficulty. Our trolleys, with all the baggage, had to be transferred to another line. Effort and energy were not spared, and the following midday brought us face to face with the first engine carrying Imperial soldiery towards Taiyüanfu. At Niangtzekwan Pass we were under the Dragon flag once more. The houses of the foreigners there were completely wrecked, and my recollection of that place is a land of feathers, contents of the beds of the Frenchmen who had left their homes, and would return to find nothing but a heap of ruins and a litter of broken glass, china, and furniture, smothered in feathers and presenting a sad wreckage of what had once been a home. That evening we reached an inn where food   warm, satisfying food—was to be had, and twenty-four hours later we steamed into Tientsin station, greeted by a hearty cheer from a friendly group, for we had been missing and untraced since we left Yutze.

CHANGED CONDITIONS

"The Master said: The people may be made to follow a path of action, but they may not be made to understand it."—Confucius.

"I have seen a Chinese graduate of a Western university, dressed in proper Western clothes, in his dress-suit, with an opera hat crushed under his arm, beseeching the goddess of mercy in her temple, with many rich gifts, to give him a male child."—Rev. C. Scott.

"From time to time Jesus was offered a place in the Pantheon, but Christianity perceived that the Pantheon was the place for dead gods."—Dr. John Hutton.

CHAPTER XX

CHANGED CONDITIONS

WHEREIN SOME, THOUGH FOLLOWING A PATH OF ACTION, FAILED TO UNDERSTAND IT

THE VERY week that the British Minister issued passports for women to re-enter Shansi saw us in Tientsin on our way inland. Those precious documents which enabled us to return to our work were eagerly received, and we lost no time travelling over the familiar ground. How easily and smoothly we now sped over the iron rails as compared with our former journey; we need now take no interest in gradients, nor fear that the train would not start at the appointed hour, nor convey us to our destination.

We found ourselves in a strange country. In place of the dragon, the five-colour Republican flag was everywhere in evidence, which by the Chinese is thus explained: China's eighteen provinces are represented by the red line, Manchuria by the yellow, Mongolia by the blue, Hi, Chinghai, and Sinkiang by the white, and Thibet by the black; the ideal of the Chinese republic, a united territory, being indicated.

Soldiers in semi-foreign uniform lined up on each station platform to salute the train, remaining at their posts until the puffing monster was out of sight. At Taiyüanfu were further surprises. No man wearing a queue could enter the city. Should he make an effort to do so, the soldiers guarding the gates speedily removed the appendage with a pair of large scissors.

The shops vied with one another in having the very latest "Republican" goods; the buttons one bought were "Republican"; all schoolbooks were changed to the latest "Republican" editions; the cloth trade mark was "Patriotic." Everything was Republican, and we began to realise that China, far from being the conservative country we had thought, was one of the most progressive.

As we came to districts where the regulations had been less severely enforced, we found the queue replaced by the most extraordinary head-dress; the hair, varying in length, was sometimes braided and sometimes held in place by a strip cut from a petroleum tin, and bent to a semicircle. The more wealthy members of society affected a style similar to that of an English schoolgirl, the flowing locks reaching to the shoulders and held from the face by a circular comb. Others allowed the tresses to fall as nature dictated, keeping them of such a length that with very little trouble the plait might again appear, for as some remarked: "Who knows, maybe we lose tails to-day, and heads to-morrow!"

The hats were even more wonderful. In place of the neat, circular cap, every shape and size was to be seen. Round hats like a pudding-bowl, straw hats, hard oblong hats, soft hats, home-made hats, erections of cardboard, giving proof that some devoted wife or mother had done her best to copy with the means available, probably only cardboard and paste, a tall hat, which her lord described as having seen on some journey towards Western communities. Women's dress was likewise being revolutionised, and skirts were extraordinary. One young lady whom I met, desiring to be more up-to-date than the rest, wore the so-called foreign dress back to front, and was far more satisfied with her appearance than the charming little lady who accompanied her, dressed in the dignified, elegant attire of her own people.

Not only had the style changed, but travelling south we missed the bright-coloured clothes which had always added a touch of beauty to the landscape. We discovered that with the introduction of the Republic, sumptuary laws were being enforced which commanded the exclusive use of earth-coloured garments for the men, and forbade the wearing of silver ornaments to women. Proclamations followed one another in rapid succession, several of which were framed with a view to altering the standing of the army. From ancient days China has regarded the soldier as belonging to the lowest grade of society; the highest place is given to the scholar, and next to him the farmer, who on account of his labour for mankind ranks high. The artisan is placed third, but the trader, seeing that he only distributes and does not produce, comes just before the soldier, who neither producing nor distributing, but only destroying, ranks lowest in the social scale. One proclamation stated that no one was to say that it was *infra dig* to enter the military profession. It certainly needed some such move on the part of the authorities to add to the prestige of the army. A few days before the recruiting agents had been through the district. "Only those wearing the queue will be enlisted" was the, to us, amazing dictum. Upon inquiry we found that former aspirants had given considerable trouble by running home when the labour became too arduous. As the donning of military uniform necessitated the removal of long hair, it was obvious that the new brigade would be freshers, and, as our informant said: "Never having left home before they will not know the way back!"

The next order forbade us to speak of any day as "unlucky." Now from time immemorial, some days have been regarded as good and others as bad for such important events as weddings and funerals; in fact, almost every day of the year is controlled by some fortunate or untoward influence, governed by the conjunction of the "Celestial Branches" and "Earthly Stems," complicated with innumerable elemental antipathies and affinities.

As an example may be mentioned *wood*, which is antagonistic to *metal*, but has an affinity for *fluid* from which it draws its sustenance, whereas the metal forged into an axe serves for its destruction.

The "Earthly Stems" are represented by symbolic animals, and have zodiacal signs and control of certain hours. Of the twenty-eight zodiacal constellations, seven are infelicitous and no one will risk entering upon a new venture on these days. To repair the kitchen stove on a day when fire was in the ascendancy might cause a conflagration, and to go to law on the day when water is the controlling element is equally foolish, for the tendency of water is to fall, and this may be the fate of the over-daring litigant. On a day controlled by the snake it would obviously be foolhardy to start on a journey, for with such a slow traveller as your controlling genius the journey might be impeded.

The calculations necessary for the correct adjustment of these various influences provide a livelihood for astrologers and fortune-tellers, but this proclamation, at one fell swoop, attempted to abolish their profession. The order was issued, and I suppose in time the yellow paper faded in the sun; some read it, many talked of it, but they still chose the day which according to their calendar was the auspicious one, and no man hindered them.

Other proclamations followed in due order: there was to be no music at weddings or funerals, only good cash was to be used, women were to unbind their feet, and brides were not to wear embroidered gowns. We listened respectfully, as in duty bound, and waited for the pendulum to swing.

Upon one point, however, the powers were insistent. The Western calendar must take the place of the lunar. The actual change of date was a small matter, but this alteration upset the whole organisation of Chinese life. The New Year season is one which ensures to the Chinese family its annual gathering, and all the subsequent festivals date from that, the greatest.

The orders were too insistent to be trifled with, and we, in common with all the government schools, closed to enable our pupils to be at home for the 1st of January. New Year scrolls were exhibited outside every front door, but apart from this, the day passed unnoticed. Instead of paying and receiving calls, inviting guests and enjoying the family gathering, business was carried on as usual. The first day of the first moon, however, found the populace given up to revelry, shops were closed, it was impossible to buy food, and the children in school rebelled at the decree which separated them from their parents at such a time, and longed for the golden days of the past. Before another New Year it was quite evident that proclamations were useless, and we joyfully returned to the old order, and now all keep the first day of the first moon as our festival.

Compulsory education was talked of, even conscription was whispered, and yet we had no criminal code, and no one could touch a neighbour of ours who, angry that her daughter-in-law presented her with a girl instead of the longed-for boy, took the child and dashed out its brains. The child is her property, and she has power of life and death in her hand.

The new Mandarin was a native of Shansi, the old rule that a man might not act as magistrate in his own province having been repealed. He was not as his predecessor, carried in a sedan chair, but walked, or rode in a cart as a commoner. He wore cotton clothes in place of the gorgeous silk and satin embroidered gowns, and when he sent to invite us to dine with his wives, his card was foreign except for the characters written upon it.

Our first visit to the Yamen under the new regime revealed some of the many changes which had taken place during the last year. No longer were we escorted by outriders, but hired for ourselves one of the few carts that Hwochow boasts. The *Tai-tais* were dressed in black, relieved by fancy crochet work shoulder capes, of varied hues. The teacups were of white china, decorated with a bunch of forget-me-nots, and the well-known words: "A present for a good boy." The feast menu was as before, but instead of the beautiful china and Eastern decorations, we sat round a glass petroleum lamp and ate delicacies worthy of a better setting from plates of that familiar pattern, white with a border of blue. The exquisitely polished table was covered with a piece of white calico, a knife and fork lay beside the chop-sticks, and last but not least, the Mandarin, to add to our pleasure, ordered his servants to bring out the gramophone, which during dinner poured forth a selection of London street songs and Chinese theatrical music. Conversation was drowned, and we were able the more to observe. In place of scroll-decorated walls, brilliant paper met our gaze at every turn, white enamel basins and bowls replaced all the flowered china on which we had lavished so much admiration. After dinner we were not offered the water pipe, but cigarettes, all expressing surprise that we could refuse so foreign an indulgence. The Chinese proverb to the effect that "A wayfarer does not repair the inn nor the Mandarin his official residence," was for once in fault—the workmen had been busy! We spent a very pleasant hour with the family after dinner, receiving as on former occasions the utmost kindness and courtesy.

The classical writings of Mencius were for a time excluded from the schools as teaching reverence for kings and rulers, a doctrine not to be tolerated in the most republican of republics.

The friendly attitude of some of the leaders of the revolutionary movement towards Christianity lent colour to a widely spread impression that republican government necessitated a change of religion. Some favoured the Protestant, some the Roman Catholic Church, others preferred the "No-god society," which gained many adherents as being more modern.

Even the Church was affected by the prevailing craze, and the wearing of the queue and nonobservance of innovations was regarded as sin by the ignorant and superstitious. I heard a new convert warned by a Church member that sickness in his home might well be due to his rooted objection to calendar changes.

This attitude of mind, happily for us, lasted only a few months, but it was followed by another serious danger when the question of introducing the Confucian Ethical Code as a state religion was brought forward. This would have imposed limitations on Christians, Mohammedans, and others, the alternative suggestion being that Christianity should be given this status, in which some saw far greater perils. Meetings of the Chinese Protestant Church forwarded petitions to the Central Government, protesting against both proposals and craving only religious liberty, and the danger was averted.

The habit of revolution is a pernicious disease of the human mind, and once acquired hard to throw off. Our political horizon has been draped in storm-clouds ever since 1911, and our local social plans liable to disintegration on account of rumours calculated to disturb the mind of the people. White Wolf, Wolf King, and other robber chiefs have announced their intention of visiting us. Our walls have been inscribed with the terrifying announcement that "White Wolf is a devourer of sheep," which in Chinese, by a play on the last word, can be understood to mean: "White Wolf is a devourer of foreigners." A bold sketch of a drawn sword was added that no doubt might be in our minds as to the bloodthirsty intention of the threat! Mohammedan rebellions to the west, Mongolian raids to the north, have alternated with the political difficulties brought about by international negotiations, to add to the sense of insecurity inevitably resulting from the removal of the very central foundation of governmental stability—the "Son of Heaven"— to whom four hundred million subjects bowed in reverential obedience.

Transition periods are difficult, and China has been troubled by those who in their enthusiasm for change have lost the sense of proportion, and sought to revolutionise much that is dearer than life itself to many of their countrymen; nevertheless, this great nation, permeated with ideals so free from sordidity, will surely carve for herself a future worthy of her past.

ANOTHER PORTRAIT GALLERY

"In tragic life, God wot,
  No villain need be! Passions spin the plot:
We are betrayed by what is false within."

George Meredith.

"Oh Christians, at your Cross of Hope a hopeless hand was clinging."

E. B. Browning.

"After all what would he have had to sacrifice had he followed Jesus? He would have had to give up his house in Jerusalem. He would have had to renounce society; but society would soon have forgotten him, for society has a short memory for people who for any reason have fallen out of it. That is what he would have lost, and what would he have gained? He would have had those walks with Jesus across the fields, and he would have heard Him say:! Consider the lilies.'"—Mark Rutherford.

CHAPTER XXI

ANOTHER PORTRAIT GALLERY

WHEREIN THE READER IS INTRODUCED
TO SOME WHO HAVE FAILED

To THE student of human nature the fact that man so often fails to respond to the highest ideals set before him comes with no shock. In the early Church men who had run well were easily hindered, and in the greatest series of biographies we possess, we see portrayed faithfully the faults and failings of those who now form the great cloud of witnesses, and are shown at the same time the possibilities of such Eves when brought into vital touch with the Divine.

The generous, impulsive David, the man after God's own heart, was capable of a tragic fall; Peter and John, privileged to personal intercourse with the Lord, in the hour of crisis were amongst those who forsook Him and fled, and Demas, "who loves this present world," is ever a disappointment to Evangelist, who hoped that for him such dangers were over.

For the fact remains that the natural characteristics of the man are strong forces, and that while Grace can, and does, make possible the "new man in Christ Jesus," we remain each in our own order, and perhaps no point is so vulnerable as that wherein has taken place greatest change.

The emergence from heathendom is a difficult process, during which time habits, vices, and superstitions cling to a man's soul with a tenacity that would cause us to abandon all hope, were it not that monuments of grace abound to prove that the power and dominion of sin has been shattered.

Sometimes the enemy will entrap a young Christian when there is illness in the home, and under pressure he will fly to magic incantations and heathen practices, in order to get deliverance from the malignant spirit which he still believes has power to torment him. Many a convert has fallen on the occasion of a funeral. It takes more faith than a Westerner can realise, to defy the legions of *gwei* which at that time threaten your home and its inhabitants with numberless ills; and strength of mind is required to resist heathen relatives who accuse you of slighting the deceased.

The test is a severe one and may well make a strong spirit quail, especially when, as so often happens, several members of one family will die in rapid succession, quite evidently to us by reason of the agency of natural laws which govern physical life, but to the Chinaman, a clear manifestation of the power enjoyed by demons whose pleasure it is to torment men. Even the very dead may rise from the grave to confront you with horrid vengeance, should the body not have been buried with full rites as required for the laying of the spirit. Most subtly has the enemy caused many a man's downfall when his unmarried daughter has died, and he has found himself confronted with angry relatives and irate villagers, when he proposed to bury the body with the deceased of his own family. By the rule of ancient custom a spirit bridegroom should be found for this girl, or, as an unattached spirit, she will inevitably return to her neglectful relatives and trouble them in numberless ways in order to bring her pitiful condition to their remembrance. In one way, and one way only, can the ghost be pacified. A bridegroom of suitable age, likewise deceased, must be found, and all marriage ceremonies be conducted with due pomp, a memorial tablet being placed in the scarlet chair in which the bride should have sat. Clothes, furniture, and presents, all made of paper, go with the chair to the home of the deceased bridegroom, and are there received by living bridal attendants. A feast is spread, and all make merry until a few hours later when mourning apparel is donned, and to the sound of wailing two coffins are placed side by side in the family tomb. The paper clothes, presents, and marriage-contract are burned, and thus ascend in smoke to the spirit world. The bodies may have been kept for years before a suitable match could be made, but from the day of the funereal nuptials the two families regard themselves as, or even more, intimately related than they would have been had an actual marriage taken place.[1]

It is easy to say that nothing so frankly heathen need ever raise a question in the mind of a convert, but severe persecution and the responsibility of every misfortune that may occur in his village will be his, if he defy public opinion and introduce an orphan spirit to the Valhalla where his ancestors, for countless generations, have never failed to receive the rites of filial service.

The missionary knows the importance of keeping ideals high by precept and practice, and that his best way to help the young believer is by empha-sising the big claim that Christ makes on a man. That claim once appre-hended will create in the man's heart an everlasting dissatisfaction with anything lower.

Sad as is the case of a young believer falling into sin, how much more tragic that of a man who abandons Christ after many years of service, allowing sins, which he had overcome, once more to have dominion over him. It is an awful reality of life that the point on which a man has most conspicuously conquered is likely to be his weakest, for the enemy plays a waiting game,

> "And where we looked for palms to fall,
>   We find the tug's to come,—that's all."

*   *   *   *   *   *   *   *   *

Mr. Nieh came early under the influence of Pastor Hsi. He was a man of conspicuous ability, business capacity, and influence. In early days he, too, had smoked opium, but when he left that habit, he became a Christian and an earnest student of the Word of God. Few could speak with such

---

1   This remarkable custom is declared by Marco Polo to be peculiar to North China.

power as he, and at any conference where he was present, eager, interested crowds would gather to hear him. Many have been led to Christ by his influence, and he seemed a man raised up of God to carry on the work of the late Pastor Hsi. He administered the opium refuges with great ability, and the work of the Church for many years prospered in his hands. Every one turned to him for advice and help, and when the Boxer troubles broke out, it was to Mr. Nieh that both Christians and officials looked in their hour of need. "He was marvellously helped until he was strong," and then, as to Uzziah of old, came the decline. Power he loved, and in the position in which he found himself, holding office in the Church, was able to exercise it in many directions.

Only God knows at which period the spiritual decay set in, which silently, and at first quite invisibly, began a work which has ended in the complete downfall of this man on whom the hopes of so many were set. A desire to increase the prestige of his name, and love of popularity led Mr. Nieh, as opportunity occurred, to lend his influence in law-cases and village disputes on behalf of unworthy men, with the motive of self-aggrandisement. Slowly but surely the material overcame the spiritual in his life.

At this hour he is no longer even a member of the Christian community, having publicly repudiated his former profession of faith. He even smokes opium again, and finds his power and influence to be a thing wholly of the past. Extraordinary trials have come to him in family and personal life, but he remains hardened and another portrait gallery untouched. The light has gone from his face, for he has ceased to walk in the Light, but as we look on his dissatisfied appearance, hope revives that he, having tasted so deep of earthly bitterness, may yet be found amongst the suppliants for mercy at the throne of God. May it be in the midst of life, and not only in the hour of death that he will witness the great confession: "Thou hast conquered, o Galilean."

There is a failure which is partial success, and under this, I think, may be placed Yen Keh-dao, who, when once he was clear of opium himself, bought up eagerly every opportunity that presented itself for evangelistic work. He had fallen so often, and been obliged to return to the Opium Refuge time after time, until new birth had made him a new creature.

Now at last he seemed firm where formerly he had been powerless to resist temptation. When he at his own expense entered his name for a two years' course of theological training, we all hoped that a future of considerable usefulness lay before him, but before that period was over, the craving was on him again and he had fallen into open sin. Another effort, and he was free once more, and then again he fell and soon was lying very ill with typhus fever. Christian men visited him and prayed with him, and he, for so long as consciousness lasted, prayed earnestly; then delirium, and in a few hours death released his spirit from the body of its humiliation. According to man's statistics, he is tabulated a failure—"one more devil's triumph and sorrow for angels"—but there are many who loved him, and who look up in expectation to see him "pardoned in heaven, the first by the throne."

*   *   *   *   *   *   *   *   *

"Puppy's mother" has lived at the door of our mission premises since they were first opened. She, according to the custom of the country, is only known as the mother of her child, so having elected to call her daughter "Puppy," she must needs be "Puppy's mother" throughout the town. She has known the three generations of missionaries who have lived here, and has been dressmaker to them all. No one has been more deliberate in her choice of heathendom over Christianity than she, and no one has lent a more willing ear to the scandalous lies circulated concerning the foreign women, even although she has seen enough of their intimate life to know such stories to be fabrications.

She nourishes a secret regard for Mrs. Liang, in whom she recognises a woman as intelligent as herself, and a match for her in every respect. It was to Mrs. Liang she confided one day that there seemed little inducement to repent and be saved, if going to heaven would entail associating with foreigners for all eternity. Until two years ago she was a healthy, sturdy woman, scarcely feeling the weight of her seventy years. A slight dimness of eyesight caused her to raise her charges for dressmaking on the plea, peculiar to Chinese logic, that old age made her movements slower and more uncertain, and whereas three days were once sufficient to make a garment, and make it well, now after six days' work it was still far less well finished off than formerly. So we have submitted to extra charges for inferior work, for old acquaintance' sake.

Then a long and painful illness laid "Puppy's mother" low, and for months we did not think that she could recover. Nevertheless, her excellent constitution did finally assert itself, and now she is walking about again, leaning on a stick and on the shoulder of a small grandchild, one of Puppy's offspring. She is curiously softened, and told us once that she had endeavoured to pray, but could not remember the sentences we had taught her.

Time, age, and weakness work many transformations, and we feel as though the veil of flesh were wearing thinner, and the spirit within feeling its way out of gross darkness towards the light.

*   *   *   *   *   *   *   *   *

Mrs. Deh had fallen so low through opium, that it was to save her from positive starvation that we admitted her to our household once more. She had been one of the failures of our Women's Refuge, and had sunk deep into the degradation which accompanies opium smoking in a woman's life, pressed as she finds herself to raise the money necessary for the price of her drug.

For three years she kept herself respectable under our roof, living amongst Christian women and joining in their prayers and hymn, night and morning, but not a trace of the softened, repentant spirit could one see, and finally a distinct retrograde movement accompanied with physical disability forced us to send her home. I despair of Mrs. Deh except when I look into the face of her daughter, the good, pure girl whose life's prayer it is that her mother should be saved. She cannot admit that this one thing she hopes for on earth should not be granted to her. Her eyes are always full of tears when she speaks of her mother, and when I see them I know they must, with strong entreaty, be pleading the cause of the poor sinful woman before the Presence of the Divine Majesty at whose right Hand stands the Friend of Sinners and the Man who was "acquainted with grief."

*   *   *   *   *   *   *   *   *

"Flower of Love" became one of my pupils at the age of twelve, and attended school for six years with unfailing regularity. Bright, happy, and full of girlish enthusiasm she

> **SCRIPTURE TESTIMONY**
>
> *God answers prayer*
>
> LUKE 18:7 · JOHN 15:7 ·
> ACTS 12:5 · JAMES 5:15

yielded her heart to Christ, and with her girl companions rejoiced in her new-found joy. A horror of great darkness fell upon her soul when the news was broken to her that her parents had contracted for her a marriage with a heathen man, and yielding to uncontrollable grief, she became seriously ill. Remembrance of the promises of God, and the resilience of youth, caused her to arouse herself; she returned to school, and begged that all would pray that the impossible might happen, and this engagement be broken.

Prayer was answered, and to me was granted the joy of telling Flower of Love the good news. "My life shall henceforth be wholly for God," was her reply. Months passed, and when the Revolution of 1911 broke out, her parents once more sought for her a heathen husband, a man whose wealth was accumulated by wrong-doing, and before any step could be taken Flower of Love was his bride. For months she struggled alone in the city to which she had been taken, and then his orders were given that intercourse with foreigners must cease. The fight was too hard, and weary she yielded and allowed herself to drift with the tide. To-day, in her husband's house, where men are too frequent visitors, she seeks to get from the life she has to lead what pleasure she can. She is beyond my reach, but her broken heart will yet, I believe, find a resting place upon her Saviour's breast.

PREACHING THE GOSPEL, HEALING THE SICK

"You make a very great mistake in thinking Christianity is a religion. It is not a religion, it is a person."— Words of a converted Mohammedan.

"Lord! how wouldest Thou deal with this sick man—in body, or spirit?"

S. Vincent de Paul.

"A sick person does so enjoy hearing good news."

Florence Nightingale.

CHAPTER XXII

PREACHING THE GOSPEL, HEALING THE SICK

TELLING OF THE DAILY ROUTINE

L IKE THE apostle of old, the missionary must be ready, however heavy the claim upon his time, to receive all who come.

At any hour of the day, we may hear the clatter of sticks upon the ground indicating that some of our neighbours, whose minute feet prevent them from walking unaided, have found their way through the open front door and brought some friends to see the house of the foreigner.

The Chinese woman is an inveterate sightseer, but unfortunately the attractions of Hwochow are not many; there is no end, however, to the marvels found within the walls of the Mission compound.

The leader of the party is frequently our old friend, Goat's Mother, the members of her clan being numerous and of an inquisitive nature.

The well-favoured Goat, aged five years, wears a brilliant yellow cotton jacket, on which are sketched in bold brush work every species of venomous insect. On his left shoulder is a scorpion, while centipedes, beetles, and other forms of poisonous insect life cover his back and chest. To his right shoulder is stitched a diminutive pair of red-and-green trousers. The yellow coat is his protection from stings and bites, the tiny trousers from measles, and longevity is secured by a heavy silver padlock, which hangs from his neck by a silver chain.

With much assistance from the Bible-women the whole party climb the few steps leading to the verandah, and exhausted by the effort, gratefully accept our invitation to be seated in the guestroom.

Tea is offered, but we know better than to press them to partake of any refreshment, for these women have been warned on no account to let food or drink pass their lips while under our roof, lest by a magic spell they find themselves compelled to become Christians.

The room is furnished in conventional Chinese style—a square table with scarlet embroidered table-skirt, and backed by an ornate arrangement of banner, scrolls, vases, and teacups, with stiff chairs on either side. Our guests' first observation is to remark upon the surprising cleanliness of the apartment, the next is to ask where we sleep, and the third is to comment freely upon our personal appearance.

"Have you turned sixty yet?" I am asked, and much surprise is expressed at the information supplied by Goat's Mother that I have not yet seen my fortieth birthday. "It is the white hair that makes her look so old," is the comment offered in explanation of my fair complexion.

Goat's Mother has brought her relations on a promise that they shall see the foreigner's bedroom and "little iron tailor,"[1] hear the musical box, and be allowed to inspect the enormous saucepan in which the school food is made, ending up with a visit to the rooms where the women read the Bible.

Before, however, these favours can be granted, as she well knows, the party must be prepared to give its attention to the one topic upon which the missionaries never fail to speak. This proves to be more interesting than they had anticipated, for one wall of our guest-room is decorated with pictures which illustrate interesting stories, the application of which throws light upon that problem which confronts every human heart: "How can the burden of sin be removed?"

The time passes quickly and most of the wonders have been seen, when a piercing yell from the young Goat indicates that the limit of his patience

---

1   Sewing-machine.

has been reached. The orders of this small autocrat allow of no question, and further intercourse is impossible, for his shrieks will not cease until his wishes have been complied with. The whole party rises, and we follow them, urging them to "walk slowly" and to come again on Sunday. "We will come, we will come," several answer, but others are deep in a discussion as to what provision is possible for our old age, seeing that we have neither husband nor son.

As they disappear through the street door, they meet a fresh group entering who are in turn received by the Bible-women. Thus, from day to day, the Word is preached and cast as bread upon the waters. Sometimes a woman will return in a few days to hear more, and sometimes, years later, in a remote mountain hamlet a woman will greet us with a smile, surprised that we do not remember her visit to our house, when, as she reminds us, we told her about Jesus, the Son of God.

*   *   *   *   *   *   *   *

With those women who come as patients to the dispensary, we enter upon a more intimate relationship. The payment of their fee entitles them to three visits, of which they take full advantage and often come under our care for a much longer course of treatment.

They are an interesting crowd with their varied complaints. A child whose arm has been badly scalded months before, and who has received no treatment during that period but an application of rat oil and charred matting, is in a revolting condition, a pitiful sight indeed. A young woman who has lost her eyesight attributes her affliction to a fit of violent temper, when for a whole day she worked herself into a frenzy, and cried until the power of sight was gone. The victims of tubercular disease, the scourge of North China, never fail to appear, some evidently having fallen a prey to that form known as the "hundred days' illness," which will carry off an apparently healthy subject in three months.

At stated periods, children may be brought for vaccination. The method of inoculation for the prevention of smallpox is said to have been introduced into China by a philosopher of Szechwan, and has been practised since the year 1014. Vaccination is now freely practised by the Chinese doctors whose fees are generally 50 per cent, higher for boys than for girls, the lives of the former being of so much greater value.

The extraction of teeth is a popular diversion, and the tooth is carefully preserved by the patient, in order that with the other earthly remains it may be laid in the coffin on the day of her death.

Amongst the number are some whose diseases are hard to find, as in the case of one family whose several members persistently reappeared with such infinitesimal ailments that we felt compelled to tell them that no further treatment was necessary. The answer we received was, that the head of the house having become interested in Christianity had signified to his wife his desire that she should be under treatment for a whole year, in order that she might receive continued instruction in the Scriptures. They thought the dispensary would serve as the best face-saving subterfuge, therefore she said: "If there be nothing more serious, will you wash my ears!"

Broadly speaking, the patients only recognise two categories of illness—one described as "fire," and the other as "chill." Their chief desire is for a diagnosis which shall clearly state under which heading their particular ailment should be classified, and we often receive a message to the effect that "inward fire" is causing trouble, and the sufferer would like medicine such as was given to her on the tenth day of the third moon, three years previously, which had wonderful fire-extinguishing properties.

Having been accustomed to the Chinese doctor and his methods, our patients, begging that the best may be done for them, assure the helpers that merit will be accumulated by those who work towards this end. All are surprised to find that a uniform fee is charged and that there is no opportunity for bargaining, as the regular physician writes prescriptions for first, second, or third-rate medicine, according to the purse.

The male and female principle in nature, by which all things are produced and which has been called the "warp and woof of Chinese thought," forms the basis of Chinese medical science, and every one of treatment must be in accordance with the laws laid down by this dualistic principle.

Unfortunately, many of the more nutritive articles of diet, such as the fowl and the egg, are frequently denied to the sick woman as falling under that principle which makes them unsuited to many of her illnesses, and while it is admitted that sleep is essential to a sick man, the female patient must not be allowed to indulge in it except at night. Milk is renowned for its heating properties, and is most unwillingly consumed by the tubercular patient, who believes her disease to fall under the heading of "fire" and knows that anything so heating will only feed the flame. Had pears, cooked or uncooked, been ordered she would fully have appreciated the wisdom which prescribed them.

All these startling innovations are carefully and intelligently explained by the dispensary helpers and normal students who take the practical side of their course in First Aid, Home Nursing, and Invalid Cookery, in the dispensary. Their labours have not been in vain, and the presence of the Great Physician has often been manifest in the midst, as weary, heart-sick women whose ills were beyond our help have found healing and, touching the hem of His garment, been made perfectly whole.

As the patients scatter, the students impress afresh upon their memory how, and in what quantity, the medicine should be taken. Only too often the printed directions are entirely disobeyed, and the week's supply swallowed in one dose, on the strength of that unanswerable argument with which we wrestled in the days of childhood:

If one dose = improvement,
Twenty doses = x, *i.e.* complete cure.

A CASKET OF JEWELS

"Happy is she who hath believed that there shall be a perfecting of the things which have been spoken to her from the Lord!"—The Gospel according to Luke.

"There is nothing more divine than the education of children."—Plato.

"The fate of empires depends upon the education of children."—Aristotle.

"Take heed that ye despise not—offend not forbid not—one of these little ones."—The Commandment of Christ.

CHAPTER XXIII

A CASKET OF JEWELS

BEING AN ACCOUNT OF THE GIRLS' SCHOOL

M RS. HSI has never replaced the ornaments she sold thirty years ago. Had she heard the story told of Cornelia, mother of the Gracchi, I fancy her thoughts would have found expression, when she lately visited us and saw the many courtyards occupied by women and girls, in the famous words of the Roman matron: "These are my jewels." The interest on that first small gift is incalculable, and can never be tabulated in human statistics. An attempt to record the many activities of the Hwochow Mission station as it now stands, would be incomplete without some detailed account of the Girls' School and Normal Training College.

The schools occupy four courts, and the ages of the pupils assembled range from the smallest, who is only five, to young women of over twenty. The Teaching Staff consists entirely of women, all of whom have been trained here, and we shall perhaps get our best view of them at the Teachers' Meeting held weekly in the Principal's room. A glance will reveal the strong individualities here represented, and these twelve young women cover as many varieties of temperament. Here all matters connected with the school are mentioned, and it is striking to see the various view-points taken. The loving nature which would lead, but never drive, a rebellious child; the puritan, who will smile at no infringement of the law, and whose stern eye has been even known to call the Principal to order; the quick glance of the woman whose type reveals an inevitable leader, the stern disciplinarian, and the easy-going, good-natured woman—all are here, their diversity of gifts revealing the unity of the One Spirit. Ling Ai and I alone know how much we have to thank God for the friendliness of their mutual relationships. As to myself, the loyalty, love, and unity of my band of fellow-workers is my joy and crown.

Thrice already has the staff been increased by graduates qualifying from the Normal Training Class, and our students have included some from the borders of Mongolia—a journey of twenty days—from Shensi, Honan, and Chihli provinces, in addition to those from all the China Inland Mission schools in Central Shansi.

The education given in the school is arranged to cover the double course required by Chinese and Western standards. The capacity for memorising possessed by the Chinese is well known. A Chinese classical scholar's memory is so trained for retentiveness that one who became a Christian was able, with ease, to commit to memory five chapters of the New Testament each day. Were it not for this capacity the mastery of Chinese would be an impossibility, for a small child of ten years old, in addition to ordinary general subjects as taught in an English school, is required in a term of three months to learn to write and recognise five hundred new Chinese characters, and by the time she has completed her course can repeat by heart the greater part of the New Testament, Psalms, and the classical works of Confucius and Mencius.

The Chinese are extraordinarily observant, and it is difficult to mention anything which has escaped their notice. Nevertheless, the classification of their observations in a scientific form of nature study is an entirely new method to them, though this gift, once developed, should cause China ultimately to rank high in the world of science. The girls' restricted surroundings have yielded new joys since they learned the delight of an observation beehive, the ramifications of an anthill, and the notes and habits of the birds which visit us. A thorough knowledge of the Scriptures is considered of primary importance, and only girls who by Christian character give promise when trained of being missionaries to their own people, are accepted as Normal Students. During the course, outlines of Old and New Testament are studied, with detailed work of selected books. The students are required to prepare their own analyses of various books, following the system of Dr. Campbell Morgan's Analysed Bible.

The many classes which constitute the Elementary and Secondary schools form the training-ground for the necessary practice in teaching, which aims at being very thorough. The first lesson, given in the presence of a critical audience, is no small ordeal to the student who after elaborate preparation with diagram, blackboard, plasticine, or sand-tray, will realise when the moment of free criticism comes, that in her nervousness she has omitted to make any use of that on which she had bestowed so much labour. Gradually, however, a new class emerges from utter helplessness into an encouraging self-confidence and resourcefulness.

A visitor to the school could see ten or twelve classes at various stages on the high road of learning, each under the control of a capable young Chinese woman, before the Kindergarten room is reached.

Here, with merry shouts, the sixteen babies are all keen to display the glories of the dolls' house, and all anxious to sing their action songs, show their plasticine modelling, paper-plaiting, and fancy drill; still possessing the child's heart, and therefore fearless of criticism. Each one covets the role of spokesman to relate the travelling adventures of the doll, which spends but little time in the house and is constantly undertaking long and difficult journeys. From this intrepid traveller they have obtained most of their geographical information.

Long hours of work are the order of the day in a Chinese school, the terms being short owing to the exigencies of the extreme climate. The wheat harvest falls in June, and it is necessary that wives and daughters should fulfil their obligations to the home during this busy season.

The month of September brings the eagerly looked-for day when by cart, donkey, litter, or even on foot, from north, south, east, and west, the small travellers wend their way to Hwochow. The babies of the Kindergarten not infrequently sit in the panniers, slung across a donkey's back, or in baskets which a man will carry balanced on his shoulder. Each party on arrival passes through the room where Mr. Gwo, a capable deacon, sits at the receipt of custom, and thence to the guest-room where a respectful bow is made to the missionaries and head teacher.

The next visit is to the dispensary where Fragrant Incense, my head assistant in this department, conducts a strict inquiry into personal, family, and village health, and where newcomers are being vaccinated.

"I hear that your uncle has smallpox," may be the alarming accusation.

"It is not worth speaking of," answers Snowflake.

"Have you been to the house?"

"A few times," says the puzzled scholar, quite unable to trace the connection between her uncle's attack of "heavenly blossoms" and our unwillingness to admit her to the school court.

Once a girl has entered the school premises it is not to leave them again for the period of the term, and all that is necessary to fulfil the conditions of her life is supplied in this little world.

One of her first visits will be to the bank where an account is opened in her name, it being one of the school rules, in order to avoid loss, that no girl may keep her own money; any found on her person or in her box being forfeited. Every Saturday afternoon eager young depositors can be seen drawing sums varying from one to fifty cash for shopping purposes, or with a view to the Sunday service collection. At the same hour the school shop is open, under the care of a teacher with a senior pupil as assistant.

"What do you stock?" a newcomer will ask the young saleswoman. "Everything," is the bold answer, and indeed the few necessities of a Chinese schoolgirl may all be supplied. Materials needed for shoe-making, hemp for making string which is required in attaching soles to uppers, pretty silks for embroidery, thimbles, needles, hair ornaments, safety-pins, bright-coloured cord with which the Chinese girl holds every hair in place at the top of a long thick plait, which is her mode of head-dress; chalk, with which to whiten her calico socks, and the acacia pod, the bean of which serves as soap. All the requisites in stationery can be purchased, and it is amusing to see the Chinese brush-pen being carefully tested by minute prospective buyers. A newcomer will try in vain to get goods on credit, relying upon her father's generosity at an early date. "No," is the answer; "come again when you have the cash."

In another room the lending library is attracting large numbers. Here again a teacher, helped by a pupil, is changing or renewing books. With surprising skill any blot, stain, or torn page is discovered, and for years the books will pass from hand to hand with but little damage done.

The range of literature is fairly comprehensive, extending from world-wide favourites such as *Little Lord Fauntleroy, Christie's Old Organ, Just So Stories,* and the *Wide Wide World,* which are eagerly passed from hand to hand—for every one reads them several times—to such works as *The History of the Dutch Republic, Biographies of Great Men, Works on Social Economy,* and many books of reference. For the translation of these, and many other works into the Chinese language, we are indebted to the Christian Literature Society. At the sound of the head teacher's gong, all business ceases, and the girls proceed to the playground, where all enjoy swings, seesaw, and games.

Sunday opens with the delight of an extra hour in bed, and the wearing of best clothes. Sunday school and Public Service are enjoyed even by the smallest, and precede the happy hour when parents and near relatives may see the scholars. At its conclusion all are hungry for the dinner, which, though later than usual, proves well worth waiting for, consisting as it does of the popular white bread and vegetables. The afternoon closes with a service of praise.

Three times a day the children assemble in the large dining-hall for meals. Over one thousand pounds of flour are used each week, and about one hundred pounds of vegetables, in the preparation of the food. The bread is steamed and eaten hot, and the midday meal generally consists of flour and water, made into a paste, rolled out very thin, and cut into long strips which are boiled for a few minutes, and when cooked resemble macaroni. If a man's greatness consists in the small number of his needs, the Chinaman must rank high. A bowl and pair of chop-sticks is the sum total of the table requirements of each girl; a cotton wadded quilt and a small, bran-stuffed pillow comprise her bedding, and a cotton handker-chief will hold her neatly folded wardrobe. A child usually owns no toy, and many have never thought of an organised youthful festivity until they spend their first Christmas Day in school. With bated breath they hear from their elders of the joys in store, and watch secret preparations for presents to class teachers and missionaries. Excitement reaches its highest point when, with silent footstep, they creep into our courtyard in the winter dawn to sing Christmas carols, and in place of the temple gongs and weird music of heathen rites, the air rings with joyful strains as class after class takes up the refrain: "Oh come, let us adore Him, Christ the Lord!" The reputation of the evening illumination and Christmas- tree is so widespread, that two small newcomers were heard encouraging each other, eight months before this event, to endure with patience in hopes of seeing the glorious sight, and becoming the possessors of a three penny doll.

Nearly five hundred girls have already passed through the school, and every few years we have made an attempt to gather them together for an informal conference; unfortunately, the distances are so great, and family claims so many, that only a very small proportion have been able to attend, and we have supplemented these by instituting an Old Girls' Guild which includes a prayer union whose members receive a quarterly circular letter.

The postal system does not reach most of the villages, so the letters must be entrusted to reliable messengers who may be going that way, and who are requested by words on the envelope: "Be so kind as to trouble yourself with this letter and deliver it into the hand of the Mother of Heavenly Bundle." The young woman whose identity is thus hinted at is but one of perhaps twenty, whose offspring bear this name in the one village. Below are the mystic words: "The name is presented inside." On the left side of the envelope is the urgent command: "Quick as fire! Quick as fire!" Thus nothing is omitted but the name of the addressee.

From early days an effort has been made to impress upon the students that a Christian community is only justified in so far as it partakes of the nature of a centrifugal force, extending its influence in every direction. The interests of students have been much enlarged by the residence in their midst of girls from other provinces, who are followed with prayerful interest when they leave us to enter their varied spheres of work. Beyond this, the scholar's widened sympathies find their expression in the zeal with which they follow missionary activity in other lands. Most earnest thought is given to the choice of destination of the sums reported in hand by the missionary treasurer. The Evangelical Union of South America, British and Foreign Bible Society, Pandita Ramabai, and Dr. Zwemer in Cairo have all received contributions, and latterly money has been sent to supply Testaments for the soldiers on active service. Nevertheless, the consensus of general opinion is, that the Moslem situation is at present so critical that all available funds must go to meet that need. Small indeed the sums may appear on a subscription list, but few gifts are, I think, more thoughtfully given and more prayerfully followed.

The money is contributed in various ways, the two most important being the school working party and the takings of the Debating Society, where debates and lectures are always sure of a full house.

The instinct for personal aggressive Christian work finds an outlet in the following ways: The annual fairs and idol processions held in the town bring large crowds of women visitors, and afford a great opportunity for the senior scholars to take their part in preaching, as also the evangelistic service held each week for Dispensary patients. The Sunday School classes of small children are taught by elder girls, and the annual Summer Campaign has provided scope for all those who have a will to work. At the close of the spring term, every girl who so desires is entrusted with a printed Course of Study, suitable for the elementary instruction of village women. At Sunday and weekday classes these are taught by the elder scholars of the village, even the younger children being able to take their part in helping the women to memorise a verse.

In order to secure the highest spiritual and mental efficiency amongst those who, by the nature of their calling, are constantly responding to the claims made upon them, we have instituted a Teachers' Summer School, to which are invited all former students now holding posts as teachers in Mission Schools. The month of August is devoted to this delightful gathering when, on the footing of fellow-workers, free from the restrictions attendant on school discipline, we meet for Bible and secular study. The curriculum of the coming term is discussed, difficulties considered, some new educational subject is studied, and an invaluable atmosphere is created.

In the silence of the moments of spiritual communion, lives are dedicated afresh to the service of God; by contemplation of the Word, fresh ideals are apprehended and more of the wisdom that winneth souls is learned, by which a band of workers is equipped anew for any manner of service, wholly at His command. The various activities recorded above each contribute a part to the up building of character and the training of those who will be the future missionaries, mothers, and teachers of their people.

We desire that, rejoicing in the abundance of life which Christ came to bestow, they may by sacrificial service gather around them many who will say: "Happy the people whose God is the Lord!"

THE TREASURE HOUSE

"Who ranks higher than others in the Kingdom of the Heavens?"

"In solemn truth I tell you that unless you turn and become like little children you will in no case be admitted into the Kingdom of the Heavens."

"Whoever shall occasion the fall of one of these little ones who believe in me, it would be better for him to have a millstone hung round his neck and be drowned in the depths of the sea."

"Their angels in heaven have continual access to my Father in heaven."

The words of the Lord Jesus Christ.

"The hope of the glory of God includes the responsibility of rejoicing. If we really have the anointed vision which sees through the travail to the triumph, and is perfectly assured of the ultimate triumph of God, it is our duty in the midst of the travail to rejoice evermore, to cheer the battle by song, and shorten the marches by music."—Dr. G. Campbell Morgan.

CHAPTER XXIV

THE TREASURE HOUSE

WHERE THE READER IS SHOWN THE LAPIDARY AT WORK

M Y STUDY is perhaps to me the most sacred spot of the entire compound. Situated in the midst of the school court, it is accessible to teachers and scholars alike. For more than a decade this room has been sanctified by numberless confidences, many too sacred to record.

At any hour of the day, or after dark when it is easier for the girl to knock unseen at my door, I may hear the words, sometimes timidly whispered: "Has the Teacher time to let me speak to her?" A welcome being extended my young guest will usually begin to talk upon general topics, and after a considerable time will gently hint that there is also one small matter in particular of which she wishes to speak. On receiving encouragement she proceeds to unfold the matter, which may vary in gravity from a message conveying a request that employment should be found for a neighbour of hers, to a tearful pleading that I will use all my influence to prevent her parents from engaging her to a heathen bridegroom; it has even been to tell me of a brother who, having entered a College in the provincial capital, is now in jail and likely to lose his life for revolutionary tendencies.

It is during the hour when the schoolgirls are at play, or in the evening when they are in bed, that the teacher will come to me who desires to be certain of no interruption. One whose father was formerly a deacon, but having relapsed into opium smoking has lost his office and Church membership, comes with her sad story. "How can I hope to influence my scholars when this sin is in my own home?" she asks me; and goes on to tell of the downward steps taken, and of the good mother who, with herself, has done all that love could suggest to save the father from public disgrace. A letter from her distant home will sometimes bring her when the work of the day is done, that together we may share its contents. How plain it is to me, that this scorching furnace of shame which seals her lips and makes her blush before her own pupils, is the very test she requires for her perfecting. I know that this is a spiritual crisis when in the thick darkness she will either meet with God, or losing the hope whereby we are saved will grow cold and indifferent.

It is always a personal refreshment when Fragrant Clouds or Pearl Drops comes to see me. A warm friendship exists between these two senior Normal Students, strong, robust young women, prospering in body as in soul. Pearl Drops, keenly humorous, is a famous mimic and I once had the delight of, unnoticed, joining an audience which she was fascinating by her mimicry of an old man well known to us all. Fragrant Clouds is a more serious type, and entered the High School here in answer to her prayers to God for many months, at a time when innumerable obstacles barred her way. She has proved "barriers" to be "for those who cannot fly," and possesses that quiet dignity and confidence which tells of character formed by difficulties overcome. She knows the "All great" to be the "All loving too," and is strong.

Little Goodness is the boldest girl in the school. She is only five years old, but will any moment that she can run away from the Kindergarten Court unseen push open my door, and show me with great delight and most disconcerting self-assurance some treasure she has found—a grub, or maybe some one else's new handkerchief. The frown I summon to my aid when the offence is repeated more than once a day, is rather a failure, but poor Goodness has had to learn by sterner methods that the teacher's word is law. It is not easy to be stern with her for she is a most fascinating little creature, and yet her parents wanted her so little that she was found, as a wee babe, buried alive. With difficulty her life was saved by the missionary to whom she was taken, who has cared for her ever since. Her most serious offence in this school, and a cause of scandal to the whole Kindergarten, was the helping of herself to five cash from the collection plate when it was handed to her in the Sunday service.

When a new graduate who has been faced for the first time by her class appears at my door, I know before she begins to speak that her errand is to inform me she has found herself to have accepted a burden and responsibility which she is utterly incapable of bearing. I make no great effort to hide my amusement, and call to her remembrance the complete assurance with which she was prepared to enter upon her career during her last term as a Normal Student. I also tell her I have been expecting this interview and, needless to say, from the humorous side we naturally turn to the serious.

Teachers are constantly coming to me for advice as to the best method of dealing with those symptoms of original sin which cause small children to bewilder their elders by the utter depravity of their moral nature. What, for example, could I say to Kingfisher who was heard, when praying audibly, to petition heaven that Rosebud - with whom she had quarrelled might lose all her good marks?

The weeping Butterfly was peremptorily ushered into my presence, accused of using bad language. I could see by the expression on the teacher's face that it was no trifling matter. She had said: "Chrysanthemum, when you walk it is like the hopping of a frog." She had thus compared a fellow-scholar to an animal, a form of speech which in Chinese, as I well knew, amounts to a curse.

Peach Blossom, ever since the first day she came to me has been a care and responsibility. Conscious of her good looks and of her capacity to secure a following of devotees, she has conducted her small court with increasing joy to herself, and annoyance to me and my Staff. It was impossible to ignore her presence, and while she was scrupulously within the rules and regulations of school discipline she somehow managed to sail so near, and yet avoid, the point of defiance that we were baffled.

I am sometimes called upon to fulfil the vocation of motherhood in a very real sense, as when I have to announce to some child who has no mother that the arrangements for her engagement are about to be completed, but that her father, who feels he could not expect her to speak of such a matter, has asked me to find out her desires regarding the proposed bridegroom. After an inevitable tear, shed at the suggestion that she must some day leave her father's home, she asks me if I am satisfied with the plan; on my answering in the affirmative her face brightens, though she conventionally begs me to use my influence to dissuade her father from any such intention. I, seeing that no difficulty presents itself, change the subject and bring her a few days later the gifts and silver ornaments which indicate that all is settled. She, having no mother to do the necessary grumbling at the inferior quality of the bridegroom's presents, comes to my room later on, and says: "I have been examining these, and perceive that the silver used is not pure in quality." Having shown that she, though motherless, is not easily taken in, she accepts my exhortation to be a good child and to be thankful for what she has, and without further ado begins her preparations for the day when she will "change her home."

The more modern parent is sometimes desirous that his daughter, who has reached years of discretion, should from time to time correspond with her fiancé. The letters all being sent to the girl's father, he forwards them to me, and the fear lest any fellow-student should know of so immodest a proceeding always leads the girl to read them in my room, and place them in my hand for safe keeping. It was enlightening to receive a request on one occasion that I would, at the close of term, return "those letters which are of no possible use." I knew to what she referred, and mentally noted that the "useless" paper found a very safe place in the recesses of her luggage!

Tragedy is interwoven with the life of almost every woman in this land. Disappointment at her birth finds its only consolation in the recognition of her value in the home as family drudge. Only as mother of her son does she enter on an inheritance of sufficient consideration to make her well worth the clothes she wears and the food she consumes.

How pathetic it is to see the efforts put forth by a child whose school life has been interrupted to endeavour to find some means of paying the necessary fees! One girl of thirteen, by making hair-sieves during the summer months renders it possible for her father to send her to school; and many weave during the holidays all the cloth necessary for their own clothes. One little girl who had no other means of helping herself, gleaned so industriously that she gathered sufficient for her first month's expenses, only to find one day that her little hoard had been used by her opium smoking father for his own indulgence.

Even the high ethics of Confucianism can recognise no higher position for woman than one of obedient dependence throughout life. In youth she must be subject

SCRIPTURE TESTIMONY
There are no gender distinctions in Christ
GALATIANS 3:28

to her father, in middle age to her husband, and in old age to her son. The revolutionary power of Christianity has established a new order, and in the Christian community we see her welcomed in babyhood, cared for in childhood, and receiving the honour due to her womanhood when she becomes a bride. I have been amazed at the sacrifices I have seen made by parents for their daughters. I have known a father, too poor to afford the hire of a donkey, carry his little girl nearly thirty miles to school. I have known the only bed-covering in the home to be spared for the use of the little daughter during term, and a man to endure the winter cold with the scantiest clothing that his child might be warmly clad.

One class, a small one, has outstripped me in the race, and graduated to a higher school to render service more needed there than here. I can think of each one with joy as in the Great Teacher's Hand, learning lessons which as yet are beyond me.

The one it seemed I could least spare was needed by Him, and since most of this book was written my beloved Ling Ai went to serve, face to face, the Lord she loves.

The intimate sympathy required to enter into the joys and sorrows of so many lives is perhaps the heaviest strain laid upon the missionary, and the mental discipline necessary to hold all in right proportion can only be exercised where there is true adjustment of spiritual vision, whereby we see "through the travail to the triumph, perfectly assured of the ultimate victory of God," and rejoice, "cheering the battle by song and shortening the marches by music."

CONCLUSION

"That Church controls the future which can demand of her members the greatest sacrifices."—Dr. John Hutton.

When earth's last picture is painted, and the tubes are twisted and dried,

When the oldest colours have faded, and the youngest critic has died—

We shall rest, and faith, we shall need it—lie down for an aeon or two,

Till the Master of all good workmen shall put us to work anew.

And only the Master shall praise us, and only the Master shall blame;

And no one shall work for money, and no one shall work for fame;

But each for the joy of the working, and each, in his separate star,

Shall draw the Thing as he sees It for the God of Things as They are."

Rudyard Kipling.

CONCLUSION

BEING A REVIEW OF THE PRESENT SITUATION

I T IS now thirty years since foreigners came to reside in Hwochow, during which time three generations of women missionaries have succeeded each other. The period has been divided accurately at the fifteenth year by the Boxer riots and massacres. The many who have helped in varied ways to make this work possible may rightly ask: "Is not this period sufficient to establish a self-propagating Church independent of foreigners?"

It would be hard to over-emphasise the need of the wisdom required at the stage immediately preceding the final lapse of total responsibility upon the shoulders of the native Church, that the move should not be made too hastily or at an inopportune moment; even more emphatically, that the Church should not be driven to establish on a factional basis a so-called independent sect in opposition to the foreigner, in order to secure the freedom and control for which it was ripe. Faith, hope, and courage, without which the pioneer missionary's work must inevitably fail, find their counterpart in the spirit of wisdom and understanding required for the proper adjustment of the new relationship, whereby the Chinese Christian, not in word, but in deed and in truth, may take precedence. It is easy to gain ready acquiescence to this theory of equality, but as was immediately evidenced when the strong and independent Pastor Hsi arose, the situation in its practical bearing is not easily handled.

A word to the intending missionary: Be ready to lay aside your preconceived ideas as to how the Gospel should be preached, how Church matters should be handled, discipline enforced, and your own position in the Church.

Come as a learner, and men who were Christians before you emerged from childhood will give you the benefit of a ripe experience, and if you prove worthy of it, admit you to fellowship in service.

In view of the preceding chapters, few words will serve to review on general lines the situation as it has developed during these thirty years in Hwochow.

The first fifteen called for unremitting effort in breaking up new ground, broadcast sowing of the seed, and establishing between Chinese and foreigner some measure of confidence. The second period has been one of reaping from the very commencement. Extraordinarily rapid development on every hand brought about new conditions which in turn necessitated new methods, so that the missionary is no longer the main instigator of Church activities, but takes his place in a large and far-reaching organisation.

The work of evangelisation and all elementary teaching require no foreign help, but we still seem to be necessary for the organisation which is giving training and advanced teaching to the men and women whom we hope to see equipped in every respect as well, and better, than we ourselves have been.

All non-institutional work amongst men is already in Chinese hands. Pastor Wang and eight deacons take entire oversight of the Church of nearly four hundred members, the examining and accepting of candidates for baptism, as well as arrangements for Sunday services in each of the eight out-stations, where the local Christians have, at their own expense, supplied a building for public worship where daily service is held. In addition to this, the entire evangelistic organisation, Elementary Boys' School and Opium Refuge, form part of their responsibility.

The more aggressive work includes a Chinese Evangelistic Society entirely free from foreign money and control, the object of which is to open up new districts, preach at fairs, and widely distribute Gospels and tracts.

In the busiest thoroughfare of the city, a preaching hall is daily opened which is freely frequented by merchants and travellers.

The systematic instruction of men, both Church members and inquirers, is supplied by means of short station classes held at convenient times by the Pastor, or by some foreign missionary whom he may invite.

With the exception of the Elementary Boys' School just mentioned, the men's institutional work is carried on in the neighbouring city of Hungtung, where, under the presidency of the Rev. F. Dreyer, a Bible Training Institute for men has been established. The students are drawn not only from our own, but other provinces, and during the two years' course a careful and thorough training is given in theoretical and practical work. A long preaching list is served by these men in conjunction with a large band of local preachers. To Mr. Dreyer's influence amongst these men we, as many other stations, owe some of our best helpers. The Hungtung institutional work is supplemented by a Higher Grade School for boys, the pupils of which are largely drawn from the fourteen Elementary Schools scattered throughout the district. Air. E. J. Cooper, assisted by Chinese graduates of Weihsien University, is responsible for this department. Many former pupils are in charge of village schools, the examining and superintendence of which is conducted from the centre. It is thus possible for the sons of Church members to obtain a thorough and Christian education in their immediate neighbourhood. The necessary demands for institutional work for the several counties mentioned throughout this book, are thus met by the two stations of Hungtung and Hwochow. United with these to form a General Allied Council to secure unity of action in all far-reaching enterprises, and to avoid multiplication of work (though each local church remains independent and self-governing), are the stations situated in the cities of Chaocheng, and Yoyang, now severally in charge of Mr. and Mrs. Ernest Taylor and Mr. and Mrs. F. Briscoe, whose time is occupied with pastoral and evangelistic work.

Mrs. Hsi still remains in Chaocheng, and carries on her work amongst the women of that city. She, in company with Mrs. Liang and three others, has been chosen by the Church to be set apart to the office of deaconess. She is now sixty-four years of age, and her physical strength is visibly failing.

Mrs. Hsi's life and example is one of the treasures of the Shansi Church. She has served faithfully and long in active Christian work, and she recently told me that she is now giving herself to prayer and fasting more than was possible during the most active period of her life.

For tills effectual share in the present conflict, for her love and friendship, and for her continued presence amongst us, we give thanks unto God.

*   *   *   *   *   *   *   *   *

Thus we believe the Church has been rooted and established, no longer propagated by any external energy, but whose seed is in itself.

The dream is so far fulfilled. More than thirty years ago Mr. and Mrs. Hsi, in faith, brought their small offering as a child once offered his barley loaves and laid them in the Master's Hand, Who gave thanks and blessed.

In these pages the story is recorded of the sower, the waterer, and the reaper, who laboured in tears and in joy.

Of the increase which God alone can give, no human record can tell, but told it shall be in the day when those from every nation, kindred, and tribe shall unite to ascribe honour and glory unto Him who liveth and reigneth for ever and ever!

"So have I dreamed! Oh may the dream be true!
That praying souls are purged from mortal hue . . .
And grow as pure as He to Whom they pray."
                          HARTLEY COLERIDGE.

APPENDIX

CONTAINING BIBLE TRAINING SCHOOL COURSE OF
STUDY AND SPECIMEN QUESTIONS OF THE NORMAL
TRAINING COLLEGE FINAL EXAMINATION PAPERS

(INSERTED BY REQUEST)

HWOCHOW WOMEN'S BIBLE TRAINING SCHOOL
COURSE OF STUDY
FIRST TERM

Book of Genesis.

Gospel according to St. Luke or St. Mark.

Acts of the Apostles, chapters 1 to 9.

"A Synopsis of the Central Themes of the Holy Bible."

Reading Lessons, with necessary Explanation and Writing of Chinese
Character.

Arithmetic.

Singing and Memorisation of Hymns.

SECOND TERM

Book of Exodus, Numbers, and 1 Samuel 1 to 16.

The Gospel according to St. John.

The Epistle of St James.
"A Synopsis of the Central Themes of the Holy Bible"—(continued).
Reading Lessons, with necessary Explanation and Writing of Chinese
    Character.
Arithmetic.
Singing and Memorisation of Hymns.
Practical Work.—Assist in conducting Elementary Classes for Women.

THIRD TERM

Book of Leviticus, Joshua, and 1 Samuel 27 to 31; Ezra and Nehemiah.
The Gospel according to St. Matthew.[266]
The Epistle to the Hebrews.
"A Synopsis of the Central Themes of the Holy Bible"—(conclusion).
Studies in Christian Doctrine.
Reading Lessons, with necessary Explanation and Writing of Chinese
    Character.
Arithmetic.
Singing and Memorisation of Hymns.
Memorisation of Psalms.
Pilgrim's Progress.
Practical Work.—Conduct Elementary Classes for Women, Teach under
    Criticism, City and Village Visiting.

FOURTH TERM

Book of Judges, Ruth, Esther, and 2 Samuel.
Life of Elijah and Elisha.
Acts of the Apostles, chapters 10 to 28.
Studies in Christian Doctrine.
Arithmetic.
Singing and Memorisation of Hymns.
Memorisation of Psalms.
Pilgrim's Progress, Part II.
Practical Work — As Term III.

CHINA INLAND MISSION NORMAL TRAINING
COLLEGE, HWOCHOW, SHANSI

SPECIMEN QUESTIONS
(Drawn from Final Examination Papers, 1915)

SCRIPTURE

What answer did Christ give to the following questions?—"What must
we do that we may work the works of God?" "How can this man give
us His flesh to eat?" "Hast thou seen Abraham?" "How can a man be
born when he is old?"

Name five incidents in the Gospel according to St. John[267] which illustrate the statement: "He knew what was in man."

Name some of the abuses in the Corinthian Church, and briefly state how
Paul dealt with each.

What period of human history is covered by the Book of Genesis?

Briefly trace the degeneration of the Individual, the Home, and the Nation,
as recorded in the Book of Genesis.

Give an outline of the Book of Ezra.

State briefly the teaching of Christ on the following subjects:—Fasting,
Riches, Rewards, and the Forgiveness of Sin.

The establishment of the Church by Constantine proved to be its spiritual
loss. Quote five verses from Scripture to show this might have been
anticipated.

Mention four reasons which conduced to the spread of the Gospel in the
days of the Early Church.

HISTORY

State clearly the advantages and disadvantages of Feudalism.

What do you know of the Spartan methods of treating children?

What do you know of the following: — Chaucer, Rienzi, Savonarola, Simon de Montfort, Gladstone, Li Hung-chang, Bruce?

What do you understand by the term "Ostracism"?

Who were the combatants in the following battles: — Crecy, Hastings, Marathon, Bannockburn, Waterloo?

Give an account of the causes which resulted in the Crusades, or in the French Revolution.

PHYSIOLOGY

What are the various uses of the Cerebrum, Cerebellum, and Medulla Oblongata?

Explain the process of "Hearing." Illustrate with diagrams.

What do you know of the Crystalline Lens of the Eye?

What is meant by "Long Sight" and "Short Sight"?

What is the cause of each, and how may each be remedied?

Give a list of the Cranial Nerves.

ZOOLOGY

Draw a diagram of the Blood Vessels of a Fish.

State clearly the main divisions of Zoology, and in detail those of the Bird Family.

Give a detailed account of the Ant and its habits; illustrate with diagrams.

Describe the Fauna of the Arctic Regions.

CHEMISTRY

What weight of each of the following compounds is necessary to prepare 50 litres of Oxygen? — Water, Mercuric Oxide, Potassium Chlorate.

Explain the principle of the Dewar bulb.

Define the term "Acid." Enumerate the characteristics of a "Base."

Two compounds were found to have the following compositions: = 43.64 per cent. phosphorus = 56.36 per cent. oxygen = 56.35 per cent. phosphorus = 43.65 per cent. Show that the Law of Multiple proportion holds in this case.

Classical Essay Subjects. — "The Path may not be left for an instant; if it could be left it would not be the Path. On this account the superior man does not wait until he see things to be cautious, nor see things to be apprehensive." — Confucius.

SCRIPTURE TESTIMONY INDEX

God communicating in a dream xix
Matthew 1:20 · Matthew 2:12 · Matthew 2:13 · Matthew 2:19 ·
Matthew 2:22 · Matthew 27:19 · Acts 2:17

As the greatest trying times for the Hwochow church persisted
with many believers backsliding, Pastor Hsi had a dream, in
that dream, he saw a tree cut down to the ground, only to
sprout again—and more gallantly than before it was cut. He
was encouraged as he believed, and rightly so, that it was sign
that the Lord will revive his church.

In Christ, believers are free from bondage 4
Romans 14:22 · Galatians 5:1 · Galatians 6:10

Mrs Hsi inexplicably came under demonic influence and
became enraged at her husband during his visits home.
Discovering a neglected idol in their house, he destroyed it,
after which Mrs. Hsi was relieved from the malevolent spirit
and embraced Christianity.

God communicating in a dream 5
Matthew 1:20 · Matthew 2:12 · Matthew 2:13 · Matthew 2:19 ·
Matthew 2:22 · Matthew 27:19 · Acts 2:17

Mr. Hsi, having overcome his own opium addiction,
established a center for Christian activity in his home and,

through the agency of a dream that provided the details, devised a system to treat opium addiction combined with Gospel preaching, the success of which rapidly expanded the initiative. His wife, Mrs. Hsi, greatly supported the effort, managing burdens at home while Mr. Hsi frequently traveled to extend their opium refuge work, which led to opening additional treatment centers in various towns known as "Heavenly Invitation Offices."

Lack of funds had prevented Mr. and Mrs. Hsi from taking the gospel to Hwochow, but they continued to pray to God for provision. One night as Mr. Hsi prayed about this very matter, his wife overheard and was led to see that she could be the answer to their prayers. With an obedient and sacrificial heart, Mrs. Hsi, surrendered her choicest garments and jewelry—her only earthly treasures—for the work of God!

Having faced personal transformation from sin to Christianity, Cheng, who once considered becoming a Buddhist monk, faced severe persecution for his faith, yet he persevered ultimately working with Pastor Hsi in various refugee assistance roles and spreading Christianity even amidst adversity.

Despite strong opposition and concern from her peers about the potential negative impact on her work, Anna Jacobsen's deep love and shared vision with Cheng Hsiu-chi overcame the barriers of race and outlook, leading them to marry in 1898. While Anna faced disapproval and critical antagonism from both Westerners and Chinese alike, Cheng proved his worth through his dedication and service, continuing his faithful efforts even after Anna's death until his own in 1915.

In June 1900, the missionaries, including children, totalling twenty-six, visited Taiyuanfu and stayed in a house close to the Governor's law courts, under his questionable promise of protection. On July 9, following a deceitful check by the sub-prefect, the Governor ordered the arrest and subsequent massacre of all the missionaries, directing his soldiers to kill them without resistance.

Mildred Cable writes effusively about a native Chinese Christian called Elder Chang, she writes of the great hospitality they received during the few weeks they were his guests. In her words, they were made to "feel at home"!

Mr. Fu was back at home one day to find his wife gravely ill. When his attempt to get a doctor from the neighboring village failed, he walked twelve miles to Hwochow, where foreign missionaries resided. He told them of his wife's condition and they prayed for her, gave him drugs and he headed back home to find his wife hale and hearty again. This experience made the Fus give up idolatry for the gospel of Jesus Christ.

Despite his nearly blind condition, which his students exploited, Mr. Ging influenced his village significantly, leading to increased Christian conversions and the establishment of a worship space, fueled by the respect and inspiration he garnered through his actions and teachings.

Matthew 6:11

Mr. Tu, a deeply religious and perpetually optimistic leader in his village, maintains unwavering faith in divine provision, frequently reassuring his community not to worry about material needs, as illustrated during his son's wedding preparations where he relied on faith that everything would work out. Despite experiencing constant poverty and the challenges of daily life, Mr. Tu's confidence in the Heavenly Father's care remained unshaken, serving as a spiritual example to his neighbors and offering a powerful testament to his faith during times of adversity.

Philippians 4:19

As the girls' school in the inner court continued to grow each term, it became crucial to find more suitable facilities to accommodate the increasing number of students. Unexpectedly, a friend sent a cheque specifically for new buildings, which funded the construction of the John Holt Skinner Memorial Court, and by the next term, new accommodations were ready for sixty, expanding Christian educational opportunities for many.

Matthew 5:44 · Luke 6:28

Mrs. Hsi, a childless widow, faced persecution instead of protection from her nephew, a problematic relative involved in opium, gambling, and theft, despite traditional expectations of care from family. Despite her troubles, she managed to carry out her late husband's work with the opium refuges all the while daily praying for her persecutor that he may have a change of heart.

Holy Spirit convicts people of their sin 80
John 16:8

After spending time in the Opium Refuge, Mrs. Fan allowed her daughter, initially called "One too many" and later renamed "Ai Do," to live with a missionary in Hwochow to assist the newcomer with the Chinese language. Ai Do, cherished in her new Christian home, came to aspire to be a teacher, inspired by her sister, and embraced her faith after a profound personal reflection at the age of fourteen.

Demons cast out in Jesus' name 95
Matthew 8:16-17 · Matthew 8:28-32 · Matthew 9:32-34 · Mark 1:23-26 · Mark 9:20-27 · Luke 10:17

A crowd was gathered as a young girl displayed the signs consistent with demon possession; she was without clothes, refused to eat and was chanting weird sounds in a voice that clearly wasn't hers. When Christians were called, they knelt down to pray for her and in the Name of Jesus, she was completely delivered and regained her senses.

Demons cast out in Jesus' name 96
Matthew 8:16-17 · Matthew 8:28-32 · Matthew 9:32-34 · Mark 1:23-26 · Mark 9:20-27 · Luke 10:17

After a woman recently delivered from demonic possession suffered a relapse, the demon returned and as prayers were held again for her deliverance, an interesting exchange occured with the demon. But eventually, she was delivered and went on to live a normal life.

Love your enemies and do good to them 103
Luke 6:32-35

After the tragic death of his sister shortly after her marriage, Wang found it impossible to forgive his brother-in-law but when he became a Christian, he embraced forgiveness and reconciled with his despised brother-in-law in adherence to Christ's teachings.

God answers prayer 176
Luke 18:7 · John 15:7 · Acts 12:5 · James 5:15

"Flower of Love" was a young lady who came to believe in Jesus. When her parents attempted to force her into a contracted marriage with an unbeliever, she took to prayers and asked for prayers from fellow believers too. And the ever gracious Lord answered causing the grateful girl to declare, "My life shall henceforth be wholly for God".

There are no gender distinctions in Christ 203
Galatians 3:28

Confucianism in China places women in a lifelong position of obedient dependence, first to their father, then to their husband, and finally to their son. In contrast, Christianity was seen to empower and honor women from birth, as evidenced by the sacrifices some Christian parents make to ensure their daughters receive education and comfort, such as a father carrying his daughter miles to school or giving up his only bedcovering for her warmth.

Walking Together Press is a non-profit publishing company devoted to supporting grassroots libraries in Africa through global book sales and through providing free library editions.

To read our story, to see our catalog, and to learn more about how you can help us in our mission, visit our website at:

walkingtogether.press